DIVORCE WARS

A Field Guide to Winning Tactics,

Preemptive Strikes, and Top Maneuvers

When Divorce Gets Ugly

JEFFERY M. LEVING

Collins

An Imprint of HarperCollinsPublishers

HarperCollins books may be purchased for educational, business, or sales promotional use. For information please write: Special Markets Department, HarperCollins Publishers, Inc., 10 East 53rd Street, New York, NY 10022.

FIRST EDITION

Designed by Mia Risberg

This book is written as a source of information only. The information contained in this book should by no means be considered a substitute for the advice of the reader's lawyer, who is informed of the particular facts of the reader's case.

All efforts have been made to ensure the accuracy of the information contained in this book as of the date published. The author and the publisher expressly disclaim responsibility for any adverse effects arising from the use or application of the information contained herein.

Library of Congress Cataloging-in-Publication Data has been applied for.

ISBN: 978-0-06-112176-0

07 08 09 10 11 WBC/RRD 10 9 8 7 6 5 4 3 2 1

DIVORCE WARS

DATE DUE	

ALSO BY JEFFERY LEVING

Fathers' Rights (with Ken Dachman)

In loving memory of Penny.
I wish you could have had more time.
J. L.

ACKNOWLEDGMENTS

I couldn't do what I do without the finest team of domestic relations trial lawyers ever assembled under one roof: William G. Dowling, James M. Hagler, Michael W. Ochoa, Timothy S. O'Grady, Margaret H. Weging, Andrey B. Filipowicz, Arthur S. Kallow, Anthony S. D'Agostino, Anne L. Mueller, Robert K. Reardon, Joseph H. Sparacino, Russell I. Kaufman, Martin L. Osinski, John C. Bonewicz, Maureen A. Gorman, C. Stacie Pathammaboun, Sylvia Galic, Scott A. Shell, Jenny E. Nilsson, and Shahzad R. Khan. Thank you all.

Also, I want to express my appreciation to Jim Levine, my agent, and to everyone at HarperCollins, especially my editor, Kathy Huck.

CONTENTS

Contents

INTRODUCTION

I n my first book, written almost ten years ago, I emphasized in the introduction that "you do not want to become involved in prolonged adversarial divorce litigation. Your life, your standard of living, and most important, your relationship with your children will almost certainly be damaged."

As bad as the situation was in 1997, it is even worse today. Having been a divorce lawyer for twenty-five years, I have seen my share of feuding couples, and even when I started out husbands and wives were at each other's throats. In the last decade, though, things have changed. Divorce wars seem to break out at the slightest provocation. All it takes is for one spouse to make what the other considers an unreasonable demand, or bring the kids back a little late from visitation, or start going out with someone else, and all hell breaks loose. Sometimes, just filing for divorce is all that's needed to set off a fight. People who are ordinarily rational and controlled are temporarily transformed by the divorce process. They become vengeful, abusive, and money-crazed. They can't be in the same room with their spouse without getting in a shouting match and accusing the person of terrible things. Some people insist on an expensive divorce trial because they want to show the world what an awful person their spouse is; they are focused on spending as much money as they possess in order to humiliate their partner. These individuals may love their children, but have no compunction about using them to exact vengeance for the alleged wrongs done to them.

Certainly this type of thing went on before 1997, but it is much more common today, and the wars are more intense and longer-lasting. In a moment, I'll explain why "divorcing ugly" has become a trend rather than an occasional occurrence. First, though, let me share a story that will explain my motivation for writing this book.

DAN AND CONNIE

From the moment Dan came to my office seeking someone to handle his divorce, he was furious. Connie, his wife of 14 years, had taken out an ex parte order of protection against him, telling a judge that she feared he might harm her or her children. Under the terms of the ex parte order, Dan was not informed of Connie's action in court nor was he given the opportunity to present a defense in court. Instead, when he returned to his house after work he discovered that the locks had been changed, his clothes and other belongings were piled up on the front porch, and a policeman was there to make sure he didn't enter the house.

As Dan explained to me, Connie had filed for divorce a few weeks ago, but they had agreed that for the sake of the children—they had two boys, ages five and nine—they would manage as best they could living under the same roof and he would not hire a lawyer. Dan had hoped they could patch things up and save the marriage. He admitted that he was in part responsible for their problems, since Connie had found out about an affair he'd had with a work colleague. He insisted it was short-lived and all over with, and that it had been prompted by Connie's growing disinterest in sex.

Dan was also incredulous that Connie was able to obtain an order of protection since he had no knowledge of the court date and there was no evidence of any abuse—he said he had never struck Connie or the kids and had never threatened to do so. He had never been charged by Connie or anyone else with any crime, and the police had never been called to his house because of a domestic dispute. Nonetheless, the order of protection was in effect, and it prevented Dan from even seeing his children.

As the case unfolded, we learned that Connie had hired an attorney who was well known for using this tactic as a negotiating tool. This lawyer routinely counseled his clients to obtain an order of protection and agree to lift it only in exchange for certain divorce terms. Connie's terms included sole custody, possession of the house, and sufficient maintenance that she would not have to rejoin the workforce until their younger child was in college.

As you might imagine, Dan became even angrier when he realized that his wife was using the order of protection to negotiate settlement terms. Stupidly, and against my explicit and repeated warnings, Dan drove over to the house, violating the order of protection, and began screaming (in front of his children) that he would prefer to "have bulldozers level this place than let you have it." As soon as he left, Connie called her lawyer and the police, and Dan was arrested for violating the order. Though he only had to spend a day in jail before he was bailed out, the experience ratcheted up Dan's fury to a new level. He told me that regardless of cost, he wanted to fight Connie on every issue: He wanted sole custody of the kids, he wanted to make sure she had to get a job, and he insisted that they sell the house. He was adamant on these points—not because this is what he wanted out of the divorce, but because it was what Connie didn't want to happen.

Eventually, we managed to get Connie to withdraw the order and try to negotiate a settlement. During this time, Dan was given visitation, and on his first visit with his children he realized that his five-year-old was afraid of him. Apparently, Connie had told the children that the order of protection was why their father had not seen them for a while, and the five-year-old had also witnessed Dan's threat to level the house. Dan tried and succeeded in allaying his child's fears, but he was so resentful of Connie's action that he began telling both his sons that their mother was responsible for the divorce and that he wanted to keep the family together, that Connie was impossible to live with, and that he felt bad leaving both of them in the hands of someone who "isn't playing with a full deck."

Dan revealed to me that his "trump card" in the negotiation was his knowledge that Connie had been diagnosed with depression, and that when the children were little she'd been hospitalized and placed under a suicide watch. After trying a number of antidepressants, one had finally worked, but every so often she stopped taking her medication and fell back into a depressed state. Dan said their kids knew nothing about this, and that his threat to tell them would force Connie to agree to whatever terms he proposed.

———

Fortunately, I was able to convince Dan not to carry out this threat or tell his kids about their mother's condition. Eventually we reached a settlement agreement, even though on more than one occasion the case threatened to blow up and go to trial.

I was horrified by the stunt that Connie and her attorney had pulled; the worst thing about it was that it had damaged Dan's relationship with his children. I was equally upset, however, by Dan's behavior—he was vengeful and abusive to the point that he was willing to cause emotional harm to his kids in order to hurt his wife.

This wasn't an isolated case. In recent years, I've represented both men and women who have said and done things that turned their divorces ugly. The cumulative result of these cases is this book. I want to make people aware of the divorce wars that are raging out of control and offer advice about how to prevent these wars, or at least manage them so they do as little damage as possible to both husband and wife, and especially to the children. As I think you'll agree, this type of advice is needed now more than ever.

WHY PEOPLE ARE FIGHTING MAD
AND FIGHTING MORE

In the past, the prevailing emotions during a divorce were usually sadness and regret. Today, anger is the dominant emotion. People are angry at their spouses, at their spouses' parents, at their spouses' new partners, at the legal system in general, and judges and lawyers specifically. They are angry at what they have to give up as part of the divorce and what they receive. All this anger translates into words and deeds that make the divorce process more costly, stressful, frustrating, and lengthy than in the past. Let's examine some of the factors that are fueling this anger and turning divorces into battles:

- **Blurring gender roles.** For society, these changing gender roles may be a good thing, giving women the opportunity to pursue all types of careers and men the chance to spend more time with their children. In terms of divorce, however, they have generated many divorce court fights. The growing number of stay-at-home dads are demanding joint or sole custody. The growing number of high-earning moms means that courts are not routinely making men pay support and maintenance (and in some instances when dads get custody, they are asking women to pay child support). Even though moms' and dads' roles are changing, they still retain traditional expectations about divorce. Thus, working moms fight to receive money from men who don't work or who make less than they do, and stay-at-home dads demand custody because the primary caregiver usually receives it. Many divorce fights revolve around who has to go back to work (or who has to try to get a better-paying job) versus who has to stay home with the children.

- **Polarizing gender groups.** I have had clients who were members of women's groups and others who were members of men's groups, and some of these groups encouraged these individuals to fight, to refuse to compromise, or to assert their rights as a mom or dad. Many gender-based groups do a lot of good, but some are hostile to members of the other sex and exacerbate anger during the divorce rather than help people manage it. As a result, some clients are convinced they are being taken advantage of because of their gender and see bias and discrimination where there is none. They fight as if they were being victimized because of their gender. Such conduct can also cause the courts to be skeptical of pleas for help from real victims of gender bias, having heard people "cry wolf" once too often.

- **Media-communicated myths.** Everyone picks on the media these days, but in this instance certain elements of the media deserve to be picked on. I cannot count how many television dramas and movies with legal themes have given the impression that every divorce involves a trial where one person is clearly in the right and the other is clearly in the wrong, that it is necessary to play tough and sometimes unfairly in order to win a case, and that divorce has everything to do with the two spouses and very little to do with the kids. These myths infect divorcing couples, making each person believe that he must be right and she must be wrong (or vice versa). If you're sure you're right and the other person is wrong, you're going to act with self-righteous indignation that allows for no compromise. Similarly, divorcing couples feel they must use every dirty trick in the book to win a case, overlooking that these dirty tricks often hurt their kids (as in the previous story of Dan and Connie).

- **A growing sense of entitlement.** Baby boomers, especially, act as if they are entitled to the house, the kids, and whatever else they feel they deserve. They refuse to recognize that divorce often requires compromise and lifestyle changes. As a result, they fight irrationally, unable to accept that divorce may mean they have to return to the work-force or sell the house so there's sufficient cash for both parties and the kids to get by. Many people in their forties and fifties who are divorcing believe that they can "have it all," and so they fight for all the property, children, and other assets they can get their hands on.

- **A flawed legal system.** Some lawyers and judges make a bad situation worse. One of the most disheartening trends is the proliferation of marginal or incompetent attorneys practicing family law. Some of them are under the same impression as their clients—that to be a good divorce law-yer, they must be tough, aggressive, and intimidating. In certain instances, you want your lawyer to fight for you, but not to the point that the lawyer's actions cause the other side to fight even harder and escalate the pain and cost of the divorce. Nor do you want your lawyer to fight so hard that the kids are hurt in the process; a lawyer who battles to prevent good parents from seeing their children or seeing them often is not doing anyone a service.

    Similarly, judges who are biased in favor of either moms or dads often render judgments that are blatantly unfair. They deprive moms of maintenance they deserve and need, or rob dads of joint custody that would be in the best inter-est of their children. One of the fastest-growing areas of the divorce wars is post-decree litigation, and these biased judgments are often responsible for legal fights that con-tinue long after the divorce is done.

Given all these factors, it's surprising that every divorce doesn't turn into a war.

DEFINING WAR: WHY UGLINESS
IS IN THE EYE OF THE BEHOLDER

A divorce war to you may not be a war to someone else. For example, some people have a high tolerance for vituperative arguments. Perhaps these arguments characterized their marriage from the start, so they aren't stressed out by the fighting that takes place during settlement negotiations or a trial. Some people might feel they've been in a divorce war only if the case goes to trial. For others, the war may be characterized as the verbal or physical abuse that goes on during negotiations or in exchanges with a spouse outside of the legal process.

It's therefore important that we define our terms. A "normal" divorce generally involves some disagreement over children, property, and so on, but it never crosses the line that separates anger from outright and prolonged hostility. In other words, you may disagree about who gets custody of the kids; you may argue about it, and the negotiations around this issue can be tense. Ultimately, however, no person becomes angry enough to threaten to run away with the children if the other person fails to agree to joint custody or brings in a therapist to testify that the spouse is likely to abuse the children (knowing that this is untrue).

In a normal divorce, people generally play by the rules. In a war, people feel that any tactic is justified if it helps them achieve their goal. During settlement negotiations, a man may physically or verbally threaten his wife in order to get her to sign a document giving him what he wants. A woman may hire a private detective to shadow her husband, gathering information about illegal practices in his business, and use this information to blackmail him. People will often use kids as pawns to achieve their objectives; they may say something to the effect of "I'm going to tell little Jimmy about how you had an affair and ruined our marriage unless you agree to my visitation terms."

To a certain extent, war is a matter of degree. While most divorces contain their share of acrimonious exchanges, divorce wars involve continual and excessive acrimonious exchanges. In a war, some divorcing spouses can't even be in the same room together without going at it, either screaming threats and accusations or physically assaulting one another. They often relish taunting the other person: A dad may return his child late from visitation just to aggravate his wife, and a mom may parade her new boyfriend in front of her husband and let him know that the boyfriend is richer, smarter, and a better lover. Neither one misses the chance to get in a dig at the other.

A war also lasts longer than a normal divorce battle. As an all-out, no-holds-barred conflict, a divorce war may include a lengthy period of interrogatories and depositions, testimony by expert witnesses, exams by therapists, forensic accountants who sort out a complex marital estate, orders of protection, various motions, and a trial. Not only does all this take a long time, but it costs much more than a normal divorce. A war may also continue after the court grants the divorce and involve post-decree motions for years to come.

In a war, at least one of the parties involved is acting in a selfish, mean-spirited, or crazy manner. This means that the person isn't interested in a fair outcome for all concerned (including the children), but only in getting what he or she wants. Sometimes, all this person wants is to make the spouse suffer. In some instances, such people don't care if the process bankrupts everyone involved (except the lawyers, of course). They are often obsessive to the point of lunacy. They say that they would rather give all their money to lawyers than allow their spouse to have one more penny than necessary. They delight in humiliating and angering their spouse throughout the process, and they hope the ultimate outcome will humiliate and anger that person even more. They may be acting in this harmful way because the divorce has temporarily unhinged them or because they are inherently cruel, but whatever the reason, they are doing everything possible to make the divorce more difficult than it has to be.

Divorce wars place people under a tremendous amount of stress and cause them to be emotionally upset. In part, this is because they believe their spouse is divorcing them in a way that will harm them or their children emotionally, financially, or physically. And in part it's because the divorce process itself, especially in a highly combative situation, involves hostile questions during depositions, difficult sessions with therapists, heated negotiations over property, and a tension-packed trial.

In short, a divorce war is prolonged, costly, and often nasty. It features legal fighting over kids and assets, and it may also include extralegal tactics, from hiding money to refusing to pay child support to kidnapping.

HOW TO MAKE A DIVORCE WAR MANAGEABLE: WHAT YOU'LL LEARN

I've tried to make this book as useful as possible for people going through a divorce. Throughout it, you'll find advice about ways to avoid war and, when that isn't possible, ways to contain and control the damage. Many times, people make their divorces worse because they're operating under false assumptions based on bad advice. At the very least, I hope this book provides you with information that helps you limit the harm an ugly divorce can cause you and your children.

To that end, the first chapter will offer you advice about how to avoid the mistakes that people often commit at the start of a divorce—mistakes that render you defenseless if your spouse launches an all-out surprise attack. In the next few chapters, I'll address other issues that arise early, such as assessing just how difficult your divorce may be, choosing an attorney who is a war-tested veteran, and recognizing if your spouse fits any of three highly problematic categories.

The next group of chapters focuses on three key problems or situations that surface when things get ugly. Chapter 5 involves how to settle a difficult divorce, which is much more challenging than a normal one. Chapter 6 looks at what happens when you can't settle and must go to court—I'll cover everything from the factors that result in a favorable judgment to how you should prepare if you need to testify. Chapter 7, on post-decree court, examines what happens when the divorce ends but your case keeps returning to court—and how to deal with an ex-spouse who refuses to accept the war is over.

The book's next-to-last chapter concentrates on special situations in which you might—God forbid—find yourself, from your spouse kidnapping your kids to defending yourself against false abuse charges. Finally, I'll take a look at emerging trends, examining how some of them will make ugly divorces even uglier and what you can do to prevent these trends from negatively impacting your divorce.

In all these chapters, I'll use real cases to illustrate my points, drawing on my own experiences as well as those of colleagues in my field. The examples also bring a human dimension to the book. Divorce is not just about the law but how people react to a traumatic life event, and your strategy should involve not only understanding the legal rules but identifying who your spouse is and how he or she is reacting.

GENDER, KIDS, AND MY OWN BIASES

I would be remiss if I didn't note my work on behalf of fathers' rights and how it eventually led to this book. For many years, I have fought for dads' rights, both as a lawyer representing fathers and in many other ways. I co-authored the 1986 Illinois Joint Custody Law, participated in many government-related initiatives related to family law, and have made numerous media appearances discussing this subject.

Though I remain committed to fathers' rights, my experiences in recent years have made me equally passionate about helping both men and women deal with their individual cases. For reasons I noted earlier, divorces have become increasingly combative in recent years. I have watched as divorcing men, women, and their lawyers have been more than willing to lie, deceive, threaten, and manipulate in order to "win." This trend bothers me for the same reason that I became an advocate for fathers' rights: Children end up losing the most. Whether the situation is a bad court decision that prevents a father from seeing his child as frequently as he should or a war between parents that has them bad-mouthing each other, the children suffer.

Even a normal divorce is difficult for everyone involved. When the divorce becomes a war, though, the damage to everyone, especially the children, can be significant. Your emotional wounds may heal over time, but the kids will bear the scars for the rest of their lives. I strongly believe that whatever settlement or judgment is reached in a divorce case, it should be in the best interests of the children. This means that the terms of custody, visitation, child support, and division of marital assets must be determined with the focus on the kids first and the parents second.

Unfortunately, despite the court's emphasis on the best interest of the child, the system itself—combined with the fury of one or both parents and the antics of overzealous or unethical attorneys—can result in a divorce that hurts kids. Over the years, my firm and I have represented both men and women where the other side was doing everything possible to get what they wanted without considering what was best for the children.

For those of you who are divorcing and don't have children, be aware that you can still become involved in a divorce war, and you'll find examples and advice in the following pages relevant to your situation. Physical and verbal abuse and financial chicanery occur whether or not children are involved. Still, the presence of children increases the likelihood of a war and raises the stakes, so many of the examples I use involve nasty divorces between people with kids.

Finally, I want to do more than help you "win" your divorce war. My definition of winning isn't about you getting everything and your spouse getting nothing. Instead, my goal is to help you obtain a divorce that is fair for you and fair for your kids. Even if your divorcing spouse appears bent on vengeance and you anticipate an ugly fight, you can limit the damage to your children, your pocketbook, and your emotional well-being, and this book will show you how.

CHAPTER ONE

Starting Out on the Wrong Foot: How to Avoid Divorce Missteps

It's easy to make mistakes at the very beginning of the divorce process, especially if you're dealing with someone who is highly manipulative, abusive, or just plain irrational. Even if you are divorcing a reasonable person, it's tough to think clearly and make the right initial decisions. Most people are so angry, upset, or anxious to end the marriage that they're not thinking logically about what they should do to protect themselves or their children from an unfair settlement. As a result, they agree to conditions to which they should not agree or sign documents they should not sign. Sooner or later, they regret their actions.

If the person you're divorcing is a reasonable person, the damage is usually minor. If the individual is unreasonable, though, the damage can be significant. Recognize that a vengeful spouse may be setting you up right from the get-go. She may make a credible argument that she still loves you and doesn't want the divorce to be acrimonious. She may insist she wants the divorce to be as amicable as possible, and that, for example, she happens to know a lawyer you can use who will keep the divorce process on friendly footing. You may be so desperate to please her and convince her to try again that you accept the lawyer she recommends. As a result, not only do you get divorced, but you may be represented by an incompetent who doesn't fight for your rights or have the best interest of your kids at heart.

At the very start of the divorce process, therefore, you need to be alert for the following reactions: denial, naïveté, and irrationality. Over time, you may be one of those people who confronts reality, becomes less naïve, and deals rationally with the issues that arise. At the beginning, though, you're vulnerable to these three common states. As we'll see, each of them can be a mistake that leads to a divorce war. Before looking at these mistakes, though, I'd like to share a cautionary tale.

IGNORING ALL THE CLUES

Erin had been married to Charlie for twelve years when she noticed that he was transferring money out of their accounts and setting up new ones. When she questioned what he was doing, he offered the plausible explanation that he had talked to a financial planner who suggested different investments that could give them a better return. Since Charlie had always handled the finances in their marriage, Erin accepted his explanation. Besides, Charlie was a tax attorney, and Erin figured that he was always looking for ways to save money.

Charlie, however, was spending more and more time away from Erin and their two small children. Again, his reasons were plausible—work trips and conferences. Still, in the past, Charlie had usually traveled during the week and been home on weekends. Now, the situation was reversed. One month, he was gone three out of the four weekends. When Erin wondered why there were so many conferences scheduled for the weekends, Charlie just shrugged and said that perhaps the conference organizers wanted to boost attendance because their members were so busy with clients during the week. This didn't make sense to Erin, but she let it pass.

She couldn't ignore, however, that she didn't feel as close to Charlie in the past year as she had before. She felt that he was more closed off to her and that he didn't share his problems or his hopes the way he once did. She had confronted Charlie about this issue, but he said that he was under so much stress at work since he had made partner at his firm that he lacked "my usual emotional energy." He promised that things would get better as he adjusted to the transition.

One thing Charlie did express concern about was Erin's emotional state. In recent years, Erin had been seeing a therapist to help her deal with what she termed a "mild depression." She had been taking Prozac, and it had helped. Charlie said that because Erin was in charge of their children, he wanted to be sure that she was making progress and wasn't sliding back into a depression that might endanger the kids. He asked her to give him a written summary of her treatments with the therapist and how she felt they were going. He said that this would also help him understand her better and lead to greater emotional intimacy between them. Erin agreed to his request.

Erin was blindsided when Charlie came home one day and said he wanted a divorce. He refused to explain why, saying only that "the love has gone out of our marriage." He had already hired a divorce lawyer and presented her with terms of a settlement. He said he was willing to give her full custody of the kids if she signed the document. Charlie added that if she refused to sign, he would use her treatment for depression to argue that he should have custody. When Erin looked at the settlement data, she noticed that the amount of their liquid assets was understated by a six-figure sum. When she challenged her husband about the missing money, he treated her as if she were financially ignorant, explaining that he had transferred the money into various offshore investments that he didn't want the court to know about and that she would receive her fair share. "Do you actually think I would cheat you or our children?" he asked her. Shocked and confused, Erin signed the settlement agreement. Though she eventually hired an attorney who effectively challenged the agreement after a prolonged, costly, and stressful battle, Erin never recovered the money that Charlie had hidden.

You may be thinking that you would never make these mistakes. Erin was a smart woman, but she was in denial. You may not make exactly the same mistakes, but if you're not prepared for the shock, confusion, and emotional trauma of the initial stages of the divorce process, you may make equally bad judgments. Let's look at the most common mistakes people make right before and just after the divorce process begins.

Seven Big Early Mistakes

Everyone has his or her vulnerabilities, and your spouse knows these weak points better than most. As you review the following list try and determine which ones are most applicable to you:

1. Allowing your spouse to convince you not to hire a lawyer.

I cannot tell you how many times one spouse never hires a lawyer or waits weeks or even months before hiring one. It may be that one spouse tells the other, "You don't need a lawyer; we'll save money if we just let my lawyer handle everything." In this instance, one person is playing on the other's fears that exorbitant legal bills will eat up the settlement. Or the spouse may say, "Don't hire an attorney yet. If you do, that means we've started the process and we won't be able to stop it." Here, the strategy is to play on the other partner's false hope that the marriage can be saved.

If your spouse has hired a lawyer, you need to hire one quickly. If you don't, you're an amateur playing against professionals. One common underhanded tactic is for a spouse's lawyer to offer to represent both parties, saying something to the effect that "this divorce is amicable, and you can save a lot of time and money if I take care of it for both of you." Not only is this unethical, but it creates a conflict of interest. The process is designed to be adversarial, and there is no way a lawyer can represent you both fairly. The odds are that your spouse has something to hide or something he wants, and he knows that if you hire a lawyer, it will be more difficult to achieve his goal.

Consider the case of Bill and Tina. Bill, a 62-year-old insurance agent, has been married to Tina, age 55, for twenty-five years. Their one child is grown and done with school, so there are no child support or custody issues. In fact, their biggest asset is the house they live in, and they've agreed to sell it and split the proceeds 50–50. Bill has a lawyer, a golf buddy whom Tina has met a few times. Bill convinces Tina that since they both know and trust the golf buddy, and because he will give them a break on the legal fees, they should allow him to handle the divorce for both of them. They meet with the golf buddy, and he and Bill do everything possible to reassure Tina that they will bend over backwards to make sure that the divorce is fair and she obtains what she feels is hers. When she requests the newer car, a few pieces of art, and half their savings, Bill and the lawyer agree this is fine. In turn, Bill makes a few similar requests, and Tina agrees to them. Everything proceeds quickly as the lawyer promised, and at the end of the process, he asks Tina to sign some papers, including one of which states that Bill's retirement plan monies accrued during the marriage are his rather than hers. This makes sense to Tina, since it was his retirement plan and not hers. Because she didn't work, she doesn't have a retirement plan, but she had already assumed that she would need to get a job and would have to start saving for her own retirement. Tina decides this is fair, since Bill is older than she and closer to retirement.

What Tina didn't realize was (a) the amount of money in Bill's retirement plan was sizable—$400,000, and (b) the retirement money was marital property and she had a right to part of it. Bill and his lawyer buddy had hoodwinked her, and she recognized the scam only after the papers had been signed and the divorce was final, when a friend told her that she'd received half of her husband's retirement benefits upon their divorce. What followed was a protracted legal battle between Tina (who finally hired a lawyer) and Bill—a battle that was more intense and more complicated than it would have been had Tina hired a lawyer at the start of the process.

2. Failing to heed the signs that your spouse is going to fly the coop.

With hindsight, these signs are often obvious: transferring money out of accounts, buying a new car, quitting a job, acquiring new clothes for another climate, conducting "research" about a different part of the country, and so on. Taken together, they suggest that your spouse is preparing for a major move. At the time, however, you may rationalize these actions and refuse to accept their implications. Even if you've announced that you want a divorce, you may still not accept that your spouse is planning to run.

Recognize, though, that your spouse may see running as making the best of a bad situation. He may have a lover and see this escape as "romantic." Or he may be so emotionally traumatized by the announcement that you want a divorce that his response is to grab what he can and flee. Some people are motivated by greed, liquidating their assets to take the money and run, preventing you from receiving your fair share.

Don't ignore these signs, since if your spouse disappears, you may not only suffer financially but have to deal with other complications. Though you can divorce an absent spouse by posting an announcement in a local paper (you still have to go to court), you may not be able to divorce cleanly. This is especially true if your husband or wife leaves with a substantial amount of your money after cleaning out your joint bank accounts. You may avoid a battle by ignoring the signs your spouse is planning to flee, but you might end up losing the war and your share of the marital assets.

3. Ignoring indications that your spouse not only is going to run, but is going to take your kids.

This can be kidnapping, and most people are loath to commit this act because of the legal consequences. Nonetheless, people abscond with their kids more often than you might imagine, and this illegal act may take place at the start of the divorce process. Typically, one person fears that he will be denied custody or even visitation rights because of past sins. As a result, he takes the kids and flees. It's also possible that a woman, fearing violence when she informs her husband she wants a divorce, decides that the best option is to take the kids and escape.

If you suspect that your spouse is capable of this act, you need to contact a lawyer immediately and take steps to prevent it. In the worst-case scenario, if you are unable to prevent the kidnapping, you may never see your children again. However, if your spouse is caught and brought back, he or she may be incarcerated for the crime. Clearly, if you're dependent on your spouse for income, this can make life financially difficult. The kidnapping can also end up hurting your relationship with your children, especially if they're young. Your spouse will have tried to convince them why running away from you was necessary, and this may make them fearful of you or harm your relationship in other ways for years to come.

4. Signing whatever papers your spouse puts in front of you.

Here are some types of documents your spouse may ask you to sign:

- An agreement that essentially transfers money from your nonmarital inheritance into marital property (usually a joint bank account).

- A quit claim deed that assigns your stake in real property to your spouse or someone else.

- An agreement in which you promise never to strike your spouse, abuse drugs, or commit other acts (which you may never have committed in the past, but signing such an agreement makes it seem as if you have).

Don't sign any of these papers without first consulting an attorney—especially the last one, since by doing so you're essentially admitting to have committed a crime. While the U.S. Constitution provides you with the right against self-incrimination in a criminal matter, it's better to avoid this situation than to have to exercise this right. Remember, too, that the battle over the issues raised by these documents is easier to fight earlier than later; if you sign just to avoid fighting about them or because you just want to get the divorce done, you're inviting a bigger battle later on when you realize what you gave up.

5. Allowing yourself to be goaded into making threats, acting in an abusive manner, or confessing to misbehavior.

If you're married to someone who is unprincipled or devious, you're vulnerable to his or her manipulative behaviors. I had one client whose wife began baiting him the moment he walked into his home. With the skill of an actress, she worked herself into a lather, hurling profanities at him and accusing him of all sorts of misdeeds. Her goal was to have him strike her or make threats—she had someone in hiding videotaping the encounter—but fortunately he did neither.

In another instance, a man convinced his wife to go into therapy in order to work out their problems. Now, I strongly believe that therapy can benefit couples on the verge of a divorce, but in this instance, the man was conning his wife. The therapist was an actor, and he and the husband were using the therapy session to record the wife's confession of past misconduct, including an affair with a neighbor and a brief period when she smoked marijuana.

Be aware that your spouse may attempt to entrap you through words or deeds. The goal may be to gather evidence proving that you're physically abusive, affecting a court's decision about custody and visitation. It may be to provide evidence that you've used drugs or alcohol to excess, that you have a gambling problem, or that you've been unfaithful. As unethical as it is, some people will elicit a confession of some past criminal misdeed and

use this confession as blackmail to obtain exorbitant maintenance payments or to get their spouse to agree to grant them sole
custody.

People are astonishingly naïve at the beginning of the divorce
process. They fail to guard their words in person or on the
phone, refusing to believe that their mate would stoop so low as
to record what they say. Yet if you're married to a difficult person, that is exactly what he or she may do.

6. Becoming passive.

The last thing you want to do when your spouse announces
she wants a divorce is to become completely acquiescent. Many
people are manipulative, and if they think they can manipulate
you into getting what they want out of the divorce, such as
money, property, or custody, they will do so. If you're stunned or
terribly saddened by the divorce announcement, you may agree
to anything and everything your spouse recommends. In this
state, you may agree to settlement terms that you would never
accept under normal circumstances.

Don't confuse passivity with being reasonable. In the latter
instance, you still have the wherewithal to protest when your
spouse suggests an action or condition that is unacceptable. In
the former case, you're putty in his hands, and he's apt to take
advantage of you.

My experience is that the shock of the divorce announcement
soon wears off, and once it does, you're much less vulnerable to
making this mistake.

7. Fighting fire with fire.

At the other extreme, some people become so infuriated by
their spouse's request for a divorce that they say and do things
that, with a little reflection, they wished they had not said and

done. Sometimes they will issue threats and escalate the tension between themselves and their spouse, resulting in a knock-down, drag-out divorce battle that costs a huge amount of money. Sometimes, seeking revenge, they will try to ruin their spouse financially or to make the person suffer emotionally.

If your spouse is abusive, selfish, crazed, or vengeful, the last thing you want to do is encourage worse behavior. In other words, if you go a little nuts at the start of the process, you're likely to make your spouse act nuts throughout the process. The threat you issue the moment your spouse asks for a divorce may guide his or her actions until the divorce is final.

DENIAL, NAÏVÉTÉ, AND IRRATIONALITY: THE STATES THAT LEAD TO EARLY MISTAKES

Just as there are stages in reaction to grief, there are stages in reaction to divorce. Before people reach the bargaining and acceptance stages, they often go through denial, naïveté, and irrationality. The first two stages may occur before you are even aware your spouse wants a divorce; the third stage generally is a response to your spouse's declaration of wanting to end the marriage. All these emotional stages, though, cause you to say and do things early on that hurt the outcome of the divorce. If you're dealing with an unreasonable, unethical, or abusive person, your initial strategy must take these negative qualities into consideration. If you don't, you may be allowing your spouse an edge that will be used to your everlasting regret. Being in denial, for instance, may prevent you from hiring a lawyer as quickly as you should. To avoid ugliness later on, let's look at each emotional state and how it affects your divorce strategy early in the process.

Denial

Deniers simply are unable to face the fact that the marriage is over, even when the signs are unmistakable. Their spouse may be having an affair, siphoning money out of their accounts, or making plans to move out, but they hope against hope that the marriage can be saved. Some clients have come to me convinced that the divorce wasn't going to happen even after their spouse moved out, moved in with a new partner, and hired a lawyer who filed for divorce. When these deniers finally reach my office, they are usually in a one-down position. Their spouses have hired lawyers and created strategies to get them what they want. Because many of these spouses aren't particularly nice people, they may also have created a divorce strategy based on vengeance, wanting to make their mates pay emotionally as well as financially. I know people who have told their lawyers, "I don't care what a trial costs. I want to bankrupt her and make her go to work for the first time in her lazy life." I also know women who are eager for a trial because they want to air their husbands' dirty laundry in public, accusing them of both real and fabricated crimes in front of friends, family, and colleagues.

Denial can be especially dangerous if you have children at risk. If your spouse doesn't deserve custody and may pose a danger to your children, you need to recognize that a divorce is likely and start fighting not only for yourself but for your children as soon as possible. Jack, for instance, refused to believe that his wife, Ellen, was going to divorce him. They had been married for seven years, and though he knew their marriage had problems, he was certain they could work them out. Some of the problems were related to Ellen's bipolar disorder, for which she was being treated. Unfortunately, Ellen sometimes refused to take the prescribed medications that helped keep the condition under control. In her manic phase, she drove recklessly, and though she had never done so with their two young children in the car, Jack always worried about this possibility. In her "down" phase, Ellen talked about "running away and starting over." But Jack was certain that no matter how many arguments he and Ellen had, she would never file for divorce.

He was wrong. Not only had she hired a lawyer and started the process, but she also had followed the lawyer's instructions regarding her medical condition. Her lawyer, anticipating that Jack might use this condition to try to gain sole custody, had instructed Ellen to convince Jack to sign a document attesting to her mental fitness; he helped Ellen create a cover story that she needed this document for health insurance purposes. Even with her bipolar illness, Ellen was in a strong position to gain sole custody. Not only did she have a good job with a major corporation, but Jack had a criminal record—he'd been in a bar fight when he was 22, and one of the people involved had been seriously injured. Jack was convicted of a misdemeanor, and though this incident had happened long before he met Ellen, her lawyer told her it would help her gain sole custody. By the time Jack woke up and recognized that Ellen was serious about the divorce, he was hopelessly behind. It took him weeks to find a lawyer, and even then he remained unconvinced that she was serious about seeking sole custody; he insisted to his lawyer that this was just a negotiating ploy—that Ellen realized she was incapable of taking care of their two small children by herself and that she really didn't want full custody. When Ellen was awarded sole custody by the court, though, Jack finally emerged from his denial.

While not all the consequences of being in denial are this catastrophic, they can result in inequitable divorce resolutions of all types. To prevent this from happening, be aware of the following signs that you're in denial:

- Your spouse informs you he wants a divorce, but you insist to both him and yourself that he's not serious.

- The marriage is dead and, your spouse moves out and makes a down payment on a new house, but you convince yourself that the separation is temporary.

- You note that your spouse is taking money out of your accounts, that your relationship has experienced serious problems, and that she may be having an affair, but you refuse to put two and two together.

- Your spouse has threatened to take the kids and leave if you ever file for divorce, but even as you're consulting your lawyer, you refuse to believe she would ever do such a thing.

- When your spouse informs you that he's filing for divorce, you refuse to hire an attorney, convinced that things will work out if you avoid "playing his game."

- You tell your friends that your spouse is only using the possibility of divorce as a bargaining chip to buy a new house or change your bad habits, but that when push comes to shove, she'll never follow through on the threat.

- You hire a lawyer in response to your spouse filing for divorce, but you argue with him that your spouse has no intention of limiting your visitation, asking for sole custody, refusing to give you certain monies, or share property fairly; based on your certainty that your spouse would never treat you so unfairly, you don't follow your lawyer's advice.

Naïveté

The last point provides a good segue to our second problematic response to the possibility of divorce. In fact, denial and naïveté often go hand in hand. You deny that your spouse will ask for an unfair settlement or lie and cheat in order to avoid paying child support because you still labor under a romantic illusion. More than one client has come into my office informing me that his spouse has filed for divorce and then said something along the lines of "You know, in her heart of hearts, she's really a good person. Even though she's asking for a ridiculous settlement and doesn't want to allow me visitation, she'll back off those demands, you'll see. She's just angry about something I said, but she'll get over it and be reasonable."

Possibly. The danger, though, is that you end up treating someone who is manipulative or even malicious as if that person were reasonable. People are often naïve about how their spouse will approach a divorce. Even when they aren't in denial about the divorce itself, they may be naïve about the mean-spirited and destructive way their husband or wife is dealing with the divorce. Most of the time, this naïveté dissipates as the process moves forward; people can't ignore the reality of their spouse's bad behaviors as motions are filed and court proceedings begin. In the early stages, however, some people simply refuse to accept that their spouse will be anything but fair.

If you're naïve, you'll commit at least one of the seven mistakes detailed earlier. You'll be especially vulnerable to allowing your spouse to direct the process, trusting that he or she will do the right thing for both of you. You'll sign whatever documents your spouse suggests you sign and agree to whatever settlement terms are proposed. Later on you may reverse direction, especially if you have a competent lawyer who knocks some sense into you. At the beginning, though, you may be trusting a louse, and that can hurt you later on even if you do eventually face facts.

Are you naïve? Here are some common behaviors of unrealistically trusting people on the verge of divorce:

- Accepting your spouse's promise that he'll take care of all the legal details and that he'll make sure everything is split equally and fairly.

- Believing your spouse when she says that she just wants a divorce and is not interested in extorting money from you by using visitation or custody as a bargaining chip.

- Following your spouse's suggestion that you transfer monies into different accounts or sign other financial documents to avoid getting hit with excessive taxes.

- Agreeing to your spouse's request that you start seeing a therapist to help you treat your depression, anger, or other psychological condition because you think it might help save the marriage and that she would never use this therapy against you during the divorce.

Certainly, if you have an ethical and caring partner, these requests may be made with your best interests in mind and you are not naïve to respond positively to them. But first run these possible actions by your attorney. Even though you may be absolutely convinced that such actions are justified and will facilitate the divorce, consider the possibility that you're being naïve. While you're considering, ask yourself the following questions regarding each of these four behaviors:

- *Accepting your spouse's promise that he'll take care of all the legal details and that he'll make sure everything is split equally and fairly.* Has your spouse been good about keeping promises to you about important issues in the past? Has he split various marital responsibilities "equally and fairly"?

- *Believing your spouse when she says that she just wants a divorce and is not interested in extorting money from you by using visitation or custody as a bargaining chip.* Has your spouse manipulated you and the children routinely during the course of your marriage? Has she said something to get what she wants, never intending to do what she said?

- *Following your spouse's suggestion that you transfer monies into different accounts or sign other financial documents to avoid getting hit with excessive taxes.* How has your spouse acted about money issues during your marriage? Do you often fight about money, with him accusing you of being a spendthrift or penurious? Has he lied to you more than once about how he has spent a significant amount of money?

- *Agreeing to your spouse's request that you start seeing a therapist to help you treat your depression, anger, or other psychological condition because you think it might help save the marriage and that she would never use this therapy against you during the divorce.* Has your spouse been a strong believer in therapy during your marriage? Have you gone to counseling together? Would she be amenable to your finding a therapist on your own, going to see this person alone, and not telling you who it was or what was discussed?

Irrationality

People react irrationally to divorce when the announcement catches them by surprise. They are especially likely to react this way if their spouse hasn't treated them well. They may respond with intense anger, a desire for vengeance, or depression or numbness, and this range of emotional responses is perfectly natural. From a legal standpoint, however, these responses become harmful when they cause people to act irrationally. In fact, a spouse who knows you well may have timed or delivered news about the divorce in a way calculated to cause an irrational reaction. Here are some of the most typical irrational responses and how they negatively impact the speed, stress levels, costs, and outcome of a divorce:

- **Violence.** Your spouse may have physically abused you in the past or done something horrible that makes you feel violence is justified, but if you react with violence, you're playing into his hands. Alternatively, he may have tried to provoke you, and his lawyer may have encouraged this tactic, recognizing that violent behavior can be used against you in court. You may have been involved in a spat in the past that your spouse has revived, egging you on in public to demonstrate how "out of control" you are.

- **Verbal abuse.** Though not as harmful to your case as physical violence, this can still cause a judge to view you as a dangerous or unfit parent, or cause the judge to question whether you deserve custody or if your visitation privileges should be limited. Remember, your spouse knows how to pull your strings, and she may choose to pull them where there are witnesses to your outburst or have a recording device turned on in wait. Normally, you may be calm and reasonable, but this provoked response may cause you to come across as having an anger management problem.

- **Catatonia.** I've seen more than one client go into a divorce like a lamb and come out like a lion. In other words, they are so stunned and upset when their spouse requests a divorce that they become unnaturally meek and passive. It's only later on, when they realize how badly their spouse has treated them, that they snap out of it and become angry and involved. Divorce can be so painful that withdrawing emotionally is a tempting option, but it can cause a divorce to become ugly. While you're dazed and confused, he's making arrangements to hide money or get you to sign documents authorizing him to do whatever he likes with your assets. Later on, when you come out of your daze, you're going to be furious and will probably engage your spouse in a lengthy and costly legal battle.

- **Escape.** Running may be the natural response to a cheating, abusive spouse, but it may also send the message that you're unstable, that you may try and flee with the children, or that you'll run to avoid making child support payments. Don't yield to the temptation to flee, even if it's only for a little while. If you disappear, you're sending the message that this may be a repeated behavior, one the courts will not look on kindly. If you need to get away because you are worried about your safety or your children's safety, make sure everyone knows where you're going so that your action won't be misconstrued. If you feel your life or your kids' lives are in danger, seek an order of protection allowing you to conceal your whereabouts.

FIVE STEPS TO TAKE FROM THE START

To help you handle the denial, naïveté, and irrationality that often arise when you're divorcing a difficult person, consider taking the following five steps:

1. **Consult a lawyer even if you're convinced that your spouse doesn't want a divorce or doesn't want to cheat you.** You don't have to hire the lawyer officially or let your spouse know about it. Some lawyers offer free consultations for the first visit, so it might not even cost you anything. What you may discover, however, is that you're about to make a serious blunder that a skilled attorney can help you avoid. Tell yourself that you're being overly cautious just in case your spouse is not the person you think he or she is.

2. **Find a close friend or family member whose judgment you trust to advise you.** Some of my clients have come to their senses and done the right thing from a legal standpoint only when a friend or relative provided insightful and objective information. People who know you and your spouse well usually can tell you if you're dealing with a difficult

individual and if you're making a mistake. They will confront you if you're in denial, acting irrationally, or being naïve. Therefore, if you have even an inkling a divorce is in the offing, enlist someone you trust to provide you with guidance.

3. **Don't act rashly.** When you're angry, upset, or stunned, you may well do something you'll later regret. I've had more than one client who with hindsight kicked himself for making threats when his wife informed him that she wanted a divorce. Force yourself to count to ten in the figurative sense. Give yourself some time to reflect and to provide some separation from the shock of divorce. Sometimes, taking a time-out before taking action can prevent a divorce from turning ugly.

4. **Remind yourself that your future and the future of your children can be affected by what you say and do initially.** This step may seem obvious, but it helps people slow down and follow the previous step. How you divorce will have ramifications that can determine whether you will be able to continue to live in your current home, afford to pay for your children's education, or retire early.

5. **Create a worst-case scenario.** In some instances, I will encourage a certain amount of paranoia in clients who don't realize they are married to an extremely difficult person. I'll ask them to indulge me for a moment and imagine that their spouse is a much worse person than they think; that the spouse is greedy, violent, vengeful, or crazy. Given one or all of these hypothetical traits, what do they think is the

worst thing their spouse might do relative to the divorce? Articulating this scenario often helps them to consider the possibilities and avoid them down the line.

Finally, be aware that these steps will serve you well whether your spouse is initiating the divorce or you are. I've focused primarily on being on the receiving end of bad divorce news, but you can also make many of the initial mistakes discussed here if you are the initiator. You can request a divorce assuming your spouse is on the same page and will work with you to make sure the best interests of the children are protected. You can start the divorce process feeling guilty because you're the initiator, feeling as if you have to give your spouse more than his or her fair share as compensation. If you're married to someone who wants to wage war, however, it doesn't matter which one of you wants the divorce. You're still vulnerable to all the mistakes and emotional states listed, and if your spouse is mean-spirited, selfish, or abusive, you'll likely suffer the consequences.

CHAPTER TWO

Different Forms of War:
From Occasional Sniper Fire
to All-Out Battles

A peaceful divorce and a warlike one are worlds apart. The former is fast and inexpensive, and results in a settlement that both parties agree is fair. The latter is slow and expensive, and results in a decision that one or both parties find unfair. More than that, a divorce war can be a nightmare of charges and countercharges, of one spouse using the children to exact vengeance, of financial machinations, and even of physical abuse.

It is a mistake, however, to assume that all divorce fights are alike. If you find yourself in a contentious divorce and falsely assume that your spouse is hiding money or attempting to turn your children against you, you may say or do something that makes a bad situation worse. Therefore, you must understand and prepare for divorce wars' many forms. For instance, one divorce may start out seeming as if it's going to be easy and then become incredibly painful and contentious. Another may involve volatile shifts, from difficult to easy back to difficult. A third divorce war may revolve around a single issue, such as a custody fight. The particular problems in a divorce tend to evolve from the personality and issues of a problematic spouse. A hot-tempered, abusive man is going to cause different problems than a scheming, vengeance-seeking woman (or for that matter, a hot-tempered, abusive woman or a scheming, vengeance-seeking man can also create altogether different divorce scenarios).

My goal here is to help you understand the "continuum of divorce." By that I mean that divorces come in all shapes and sizes, and it will benefit you to know them all, from the easiest to the most difficult. Too often, people don't realize that the run-of-the-mill bickering that characterizes some divorces is nothing compared to how vituperative the divorce could be. As much as is possible, you want to keep or shift your divorce from the side of the continuum where bitter argument is as bad as it gets. If you understand that continuum—if you're aware of how ugly a divorce can get—you're motivated to do everything possible to limit the scope of the war. I've found that divorcing couples escalate wars out of control when they're operating out of ignorance—when they don't know or consider the consequences of filing for false orders of protection or harassing a spouse by hiring a private eye to follow her around in an intimidating manner. It's not what you know that will hurt you during a divorce, but what you don't know.

It also helps to have a positive incentive to make the divorce as easy as possible, and to that end, let me share a description of the ideal divorce and its variations.

THE IDEAL:
BREAKING UP CAN BE EASY TO DO

By definition, divorce is not a pleasant experience. You're ending a relationship that began with high expectations, one that also may have produced children and a sizable estate. Ending the relationship means opening old wounds (not to mention new ones) and trying to reach agreement with a spouse with whom you don't see eye to eye. So even in the best of circumstances, the concept of an easy or ideal divorce is relative.

Nonetheless, it is possible. Some divorces are easy because people haven't been married for long, have accumulated few assets, and have no children. The odds are, though, you wouldn't have picked up this book if this described your divorce situation.

Therefore, let's start out considering the ideal divorce given at least one child, a marriage of a certain length (five years or more), and a moderate amount of assets (a house or condo, some savings, a retirement plan, and some stocks). Let us assume from the start that both people are reasonable and concerned with the best interests of their kids. Though they may have fought during the marriage and one or both of them realized that the relationship was no longer working, they go into the divorce with a desire to make the best of a bad situation.

In certain instances, they can end the relationship without lawyers, using a mediator as well as do-it-yourself books, software, and articles. Both parties meet with the mediator, who helps them agree about everything from division of assets to custody to visitation. Assuming both parties have agreed on these issues in advance and are able to handle the legal paperwork, the process is a breeze, with little or no emotional upset. The divorce may take as little as a week or two in most states and cost less than $2,000.

Be aware, however, that though this may sound ideal, it is often unrealistic if there are children or substantial assets involved. It is generally advisable for both parties to have their own lawyers. If both parties really are in agreement about the major issues, representation by attorneys is cheap insurance. The attorneys' fees won't be significant if the divorce is amicable and terms are agreed to quickly. More important, a highly skilled family law attorney should be able to make sure that you're receiving a fair settlement and not making a blunder that can have you going back to post-decree court for years to come. If you have a difficult spouse and don't know it, you may be manipulated during this process. This spouse may take advantage of your desire to avoid causing your child any emotional upset and suggest terms that are unfair, but couch them in a way that seems to be the right thing for your child. You may not be thinking clearly—a common state for people when their spouse's desire for divorce catches them unaware—and you may need an advocate to point out the potential problems with what you're agreeing to.

So let's modify the ideal divorce by assuming that both you and your spouse have legal representation. Let us further assume that you've been married for a while, have children, and have accumulated assets that are in six figures. To make it even more challenging to achieve an ideal divorce, let's say that one of you wants the divorce but the other doesn't; the spouse who doesn't want it is very angry and confused. Even with this scenario, if both parties and their lawyers try to be reasonable, the divorce process can be tolerable. It may not be easy, however, because a significant amount of assets complicates matters. The process may slow down a bit, since experts often must determine a value for these assets so they can be divided fairly. You may also require mediation, especially if one person remains upset about the divorce; in these situations, it's advisable that you find a mediator who is also a therapist. Bringing in such an individual to help the couple reach an accord may add a bit of time, but the divorce can still move with speed and without rancor.

With the mediator's help, the couple may quickly agree on the major points of the divorce settlement. Though they may quibble about a few possessions, they don't fight about most issues since the valuations were fair and thorough. No costly and time-consuming depositions need to be taken; written interrogatories (questions posed by lawyers to each party and answered in writing) suffice. The parties are also of one mind about custody, child support payments, and visitation. Within a matter of weeks they have reached a verbal settlement, and in another week or so the lawyers have it in writing; there is no need to go to court and litigate the issues. After the settlement is final, neither party ever returns to post-decree court to attack or modify it.

This ideal scenario sounds so reasonable, it's difficult to believe that more people don't follow it. Unfortunately, one difficult person can shatter this ideal. Let's examine the various ways that a divorce becomes problematic, starting with minor bumps in the road and going all the way down to ditches and dead ends.

DEGREES OF DIFFICULTY

The following are just some of the ways a divorce can become more expensive, emotionally traumatic, and contentious than normal. Though I'm listing these actions in increasing order of severity, be aware that even the lowest degree of difficulty may cause you major problems. For example, one person may drag his feet initially about getting the divorce, which is irritating but manageable. Another individual may drag his feet to the point that you have to put your life on hold, the children are suffering emotionally and financially, and you feel like you're stuck in limbo. In addition, the more of the following list that applies to your spouse and your situation, the more difficult the divorce tends to be. With these provisos in mind, let's look at what people do to make divorce increasingly ugly and some ways you might respond to make it less so.

Drag their feet

People can delay divorces in innumerable ways. Generally, once you file, your spouse has thirty days to appear and respond after being legally served with notice of the divorce. If your spouse fails to make an appearance and respond within this time, a default judgment can be entered against her and she can lose everything. Some people, though, are very successful at prolonging the process. Your spouse may honestly believe that a divorce is a mistake and delay it at first by convincing you to dismiss your petition for a divorce or by hiring an attorney and engaging in preliminary delaying tactics. Once your spouse is convinced that you want a divorce and won't change your mind, she may cease using these delaying tactics.

Other people, however, want to drag out the process for as long as possible, primarily to aggravate their spouse. This is especially true if your spouse is the primary wage earner and knows extending the process will cause you significant financial hardship. It may also be that she is well aware of your desire to end the marriage as quickly as possible so you can get on with your life; that awareness causes her to drag things out with agonizing slowness. Her attorney may ask the court for multiple continuances based on all sorts of grounds, both real and fabricated—illness, work situations, travel requirements, school terms, and so on. In addition, the process can be extended if your spouse decides that numerous nonparty depositions (of the neighbors, teachers, relatives, babysitters, and work colleagues) must be taken and multiple experts (accountants, financial planners, therapists, doctors, and so on) must be consulted as well.

Respond to an impending divorce with anger, argument, and guilt-inducing actions

These responses are tough to take emotionally, but to a certain extent they should be expected. Your spouse is more likely to give you grief if you initiate divorce proceedings, but may be furious even if he's the one who files for divorce; he may feel that you've made his life miserable or that you've done something that is unforgivable, so his righteous indignation makes it irrelevant who filed the papers. Be aware that the early stages of the divorce process can be a highly emotional time when people say things they don't mean or act in unusual or uncharacteristic ways. No doubt, this is a difficult period, but it doesn't have to lead to a major fight.

Don't overreact to what may be temporary emotional upset. Divorces "blow up" legally when one person responds to anger with even greater anger, creating an escalating war of attrition that otherwise would have been a brief skirmish. In addition, some people feel so guilty that they give in to their spouse's unreasonable demands, agreeing to terms that aren't fair. Therefore, allow a bit of time to pass before you do anything. Your spouse may settle down after blowing off some steam, and you can continue to move forward in a reasonable manner.

Serve their spouse with papers in embarrassing places

People who file for divorce have three options for starting the process. They can request their spouse voluntarily file an appearance with the court; they can ask their spouse to voluntarily accept service of the court papers; or they can have a court-appointed process server or law enforcement officer serve these papers on their spouse. Having an officer of the law serve people at their home or business should be reserved for cases where they refuse to file an appearance or accept service of process, or when great conflict exists between the two parties. There is nothing more embarrassing than having a police officer serve you with papers at work, and nothing more unnerving than hearing the doorbell ring at 11:00 A.M. and seeing a policeman at the door (and having your neighbors see him as well).

If your spouse uses this tactic to provoke you, remain calm. As obnoxious as it might be, this approach has no bearing on the case and may well represent aberrant behavior, a result of your spouse's intense but temporary anger. Similarly, don't you use this tactic if you're furious with your spouse; being served at work can become an excuse for your spouse to do something equally nasty to you.

Depose the spouse, friends, family, colleagues, and neighbors in a particularly loathsome manner

Written interrogatories of parties and witness statements of nonparties are often a better option than depositions and are fine for relatively amicable divorces. Interrogatories consist of written questions that you can answer in writing where you please; your attorney mails your responses back to the opposing attorney. These written interrogatories generally avoid the emotional minefields that can be easily detonated during a deposition. Not only is it more painful responding in person to questions about your marriage with a court reporter present, but the opposing attorney may ask questions designed to provoke you ("How many times did you cheat on your spouse besides the one your spouse knows about?"). Taking depositions of other people you know will irritate them; and they may let you know they're irritated; this is the primary purpose of the exercise, rather than unearthing information for use in the case.

Sometimes, however, depositions are necessary. When serious conflicts and deceptions exist about important issues, such as custody, depositions are often more useful for obtaining the truth. Many times, people are "coached" by their attorneys on how to answer written interrogatories. Coaching is more difficult when the questions are asked in person, and people may say things during their depositions that help the attorney make a more convincing case.

Use the children to send messages

Both moms and dads may use their children directly or indirectly during the divorce process to enrage their spouse or make them feel guilty. For example, one mom may tell her kids to communicate to their dad that they don't have enough money to live on, and that his unwillingness to give them enough money before the divorce is final means they have only beans and rice to eat for dinner every night. A dad may tell his kids that he is feeling depressed or even suicidal because of their mother's desire for a divorce. Both are using the children to exacerbate the guilt they probably feel simply because they initiated the divorce. I have known clients whose children have asked them, "Why are you being so mean to Mom (or Dad)? She told us that she still loves you despite all the terrible things you've done."

In other instances, people mention something when their kids are around that they know will get back to their spouse through the children. One parent may mention that he's happier now than he's ever been, or that he has finally met someone with whom he's fallen in love. Some parents also use their children in ways designed to drive their spouses crazy. I know one man who, when he had his kids on the weekends, allowed them to eat as many sweets and drink as much caffeinated soda as they wanted and to stay up late watching R-rated movies on cable, and told them not to worry about doing their homework. When he returned the kids to his wife, they were hyper, bone-tired, and ill-prepared for school.

Again, these infuriating or guilt-inducing tactics can cause you to overreact and ratchet up the level of tension between you and your spouse, and to turn personal skirmishes into all-out legal battles.

Argue about who gets what

In most divorces where couples have been married for a number of years, disputes about property arise. Sometimes these are perfectly understandable; both people love a particular painting that they purchased when they were in Europe, for instance. A certain amount of negotiation is part of the process, and one person may have to sacrifice the painting in exchange for receiving a sculpture or other art object.

These arguments, however, can become completely irrational and vengeance-based. Your spouse may care nothing about that painting you love, but he may insist that he wants it just to aggravate you. I have heard more than one client declare, "I would rather incur ten times in legal fees what the painting costs than allow her to have it." Your spouse may also use specific objects as bargaining chips; for instance: "I'm going to make it as difficult as possible for you to see our daughter unless you give me the BMW."

These types of arguments can be draining emotionally (not to mention financially), but it helps to recognize that no matter how your spouse uses these objects in the bargaining process, the court generally divides property fairly if the case is presented correctly.

Use superior financial resources to make their spouse sweat

In many divorcing relationships, one person has a significant financial advantage. This person may be the only working parent, make more money, or have wealthy parents or an inheritance. In these instances, a difficult person can cause his spouse much grief by making the process more complex than it has to be. By refusing to settle and insisting on going to court, he causes the costs to skyrocket. By calling in experts to testify on his behalf, he forces the other party to bring in her own experts. By turning the courtroom into a circus where everyone from family members to doctors to financial analysts testifies, he turns the divorce into an unbearable expense.

Enraged, jealous, vengeful, or abusive people aren't rational, and a spouse who is using this tactic probably doesn't care how much it's costing him or that the court may make him pay later rather than sooner—or both! If you can't calm down your spouse and demonstrate that ultimately, your children are suffering financially as well as yourself because of such behavior, then you simply must dig in until the court hands down a judgment. Sooner or later, the financial torture will end. In the interim, don't do anything to show your spouse that these financial tactics are getting to you. Psychological warfare is often waged beneath the surface of legal attacks and counterattacks, and you should not allow your spouse to realize that these financial machinations are having an effect.

Use the children as pawns in the game

Threatening to limit or deny visitation is a powerful threat, and it can terrify a parent who loves his children. Whether or not it's an empty threat is irrelevant. When a spouse tells you that she's never going to let you see your children again or that she's going to lie under oath to make sure you never see them again, you're petrified. Often, parents who are the primary caregivers but lack financial resources feel they must play the child card—that they must use this threat to gain sufficient financial support.

As difficult as these threats can make the process, don't respond in kind. Don't issue threats of your own and create a cold-war showdown. Instead, recognize that in most cases, the truth will come out. In other words, if you've been a good, responsible parent, your spouse cannot deny you a chance to see your kids on a regular basis. More to the point, the court won't allow it in most instances.

Hire a private eye to spy on their spouse

As you'll see later, private detectives have a place in the process. Sometimes, however, a divorcing person (and his lawyer) uses them for harassment purposes. It is unnerving to see a private eye with a camera hanging around your office or outside of your home; it is uncomfortable to look in your car's rearview mirror and realize you're being followed. Even if you're not guilty of anything, it makes you feel guilty or at least paranoid that even the slightest slip—a cross word said to your child on an outing to the zoo—will be used against you.

As unpleasant as it is to be spied upon, if you are a decent person and aren't hiding money, guilty of criminal activities, or doing anything else illegal, don't let this unpleasant but ultimately benign spying unhinge you.

Use verbal abuse

Just about everyone who gets divorced argues. Not everyone, however, engages in continuous verbal battles where threats and vile accusations become routine forms of communication. A spouse may be so furious that he's being divorced or so enraged at what he feels has been ill treatment for the entire length of the marriage that he may let loose a barrage of insults that devastates his partner. Being on the receiving end of this abuse is demoralizing, especially if your children are present when it occurs. This abuse can also be frightening, especially when the threats raise the possibility of physical harm to you or the children.

You need to discuss any threats of this type with your attorney, who can advise you on how to deal with them. Even if the verbal abuse stops short of these threats, you still may be able to obtain a court order restraining or enjoining your spouse from such conduct. If you obtain such an order and it is violated, your spouse is subject to incarceration.

Hide money

This is a despicable act, and it can cause real financial hardship for you and your children if your spouse gets away with it. Here is one possible scenario. John hires a Swiss lawyer and forms a corporation with $1 million, but puts only 5 percent of the stock in his name, with the remainder in bearer stock. This bearer stock is then placed in a safe-deposit box in a Swiss bank. This way he may feel safe with stock valued at only $50,000 in his name. This entails a certain amount of risk for John—he needs a collaborator—but he may feel it's worth the risk to prevent his spouse from getting her hands on 95 percent of the money. John's risk is that his cohort in Switzerland may end up relieving him of that $950,000.

People will go to extraordinary lengths to deprive their spouses of money that is rightfully due to them in a divorce. Tom, for instance, managed to liquidate a number of assets, turn them into six figures in cash, and buy houses in a collapsed housing market for about $25,000 each. He put the homes in his girlfriend's name, guaranteeing that his wife couldn't get at the money. His tactic backfired, however, when his girlfriend sold the houses and skipped town, never to be seen again by Tom.

Financial revenge usually ends up devastating both parties. As my father once told me, when you dig a hole for revenge, you need to dig two—the second one is for you.

Use a court proceeding to humiliate and upset their spouse

Your spouse may not even care about custody or financial issues. All she wants is a chance to air what she feels is your bad behavior in public. She wants the world to know about your extramarital affairs, your drinking problem, how you gambled away the family's money, and your insane jealousy. As a result, she may subpoena friends, family members, work colleagues, and others to testify in court. She may mail transcripts of the courts proceedings to everyone you know.

Accuse their spouse of illegal drug use, child abuse, or other criminal acts

Many times, furious people manufacture these charges and justify it to themselves. They tell themselves, "She deserves it; even if she didn't do it, she thought about it," or "I don't know if he's been abusive, but I bet that he would be under the right circumstances." In other instances, someone will goad her spouse into striking her. She may use ancient history—a pot bust when the spouse was nineteen years old—to create problems.

Your spouse knows you better than anyone else in the world, especially your vulnerabilities and past indiscretions, and you can count on them being used against you if your spouse is sufficiently angry or provoked. If you ever were treated for a drug or alcohol problem, were a member of a cult, or were arrested for even a misdemeanor, your spouse may blow up that past action into a present problem. A savvy lawyer can take this flimsy "evidence" and use it against you as the divorce proceeds. An order of protection may be entered against you, or you may be allowed to visit your children only under supervision.

Use physical abuse

If this occurs, you should immediately pursue an order of protection and attempt to gather as much evidence as you can to document this abuse. If, for instance, you're treated at a hospital for injuries sustained by your spouse's attack, make sure your attorney gathers this evidence and uses it when asking for an order of protection. Similarly, have photos taken of your injuries. If there are witnesses, ask them to testify on your behalf.

Abscond with the children

This is rare, but it does happen. A spouse who believes—rightly or wrongly—that he is going to be denied custody or prevented from seeing his children regularly or at all may be tempted to kidnap them and run. Therefore, if your spouse makes this threat, don't take it lightly. Tell your lawyer about it immediately. Even if such a threat isn't made, you need to be aware of whether your spouse is capable of this extreme action and take the correct legal steps to prevent it.

Keep the divorce going for years

When you're dealing with certain types of difficult people, the divorce is never final. Post-decree court is an option they exercise regularly to inflict pain. Whatever the court-mandated terms of the settlement, they frequently try to change the terms. They change jobs or lose their jobs and file post-decree pleadings to decrease or abate their child support or maintenance payments. They complain that during visitation their spouse is saying negative things about them that are harming their relationship with the kids. They demand that all the terms be changed now that their spouse has remarried.

Even though this last item isn't as bad as physical abuse or some of the other repercussions of divorce wars, it can create the highest possible levels of stress. When the divorce becomes final, people assume they can finally breathe easier. They are then shocked and outraged to discover that a difficult spouse can create unpleasantness for years to come by requesting changes to the divorce terms.

EVERY DIVORCE IS UNIQUELY DIFFICULT

Even though the previous degrees of difficulty were listed in approximate order of magnitude, they may not reflect the degrees of difficulty you're experiencing. Your spouse, for instance, may simply be dragging his feet—a low degree of difficulty on our ranking—but doing so in ways that drive you absolutely nuts. His evasiveness is causing you and your kids tremendous financial difficulty, and all his excuses about why it is not a good time for a divorce are preventing a relationship you've established with another man from moving forward. To you, therefore, this is an incredibly difficult divorce. It may cause you to say or do things that prompt your spouse to stop dragging his feet but express his hostility in different ways—demanding sole custody, perhaps, refusing to agree to pay any maintenance, or accusing you of harming your children psychologically because of your new relationship. In very short order, the divorce can become extremely ugly.

Another person may be married to someone who is threatening him with severely limited visitation and has leveled all sorts of false charges against him, but he is handling the situation with equanimity, having faith in his lawyer and in the legal system to make things right.

Therefore, take the previous degrees of difficulty with a grain of salt. Your divorce may become a financially and emotionally draining battle for reasons I haven't mentioned or have merely touched on. What I've found over the years is that the real horror stories—the cases of exceptional cruelty or financial chicanery—tend to be unique, an outgrowth of a particular person's obsessions or mental instability. For instance, Terry is a business executive who was married to Margaret for twenty-three years; they have two daughters: Tina, eighteen and Denise, twenty-one. Margaret felt Terry was stifling her growth and suffocating her, and she told him she wanted a divorce. Neither one was having an affair, nor were there any significant financial issues. Though Terry still loved Margaret, he recognized that the relationship was not what it once had been and agreed that the divorce made sense. The process went relatively smoothly and terms were agreed to, but Margaret became increasingly and inexplicably angry with Terry in the weeks leading up to the divorce. Unbeknownst to Terry, Margaret had been telling their daughters about his "mental cruelty" during the years of their marriage and all the negative things he had said about Tina and Denise—none of which were true. Nonetheless, Margaret's character assassination had its intended effect, and Terry's two daughters grew estranged from him.

Both Tina and Denise went to college out of state, and Margaret moved to the city where their college was located but didn't tell Terry where she had moved. According to the divorce decree, Terry was obligated to pay for his daughters' college education, and he did so until Margaret moved and stopped sending invoices or Tina's and Denise's transcripts. Terry wanted the invoices to keep track of what he was paying for, and he was entitled to see his daughters' grades. Terry kept asking for the invoices and grade reports, Margaret kept refusing, their arguments via phone and e-mail escalated, and finally Terry refused to pay for his daughters' education until Margaret sent him what he requested. Margaret immediately requested and received an order of protection, and Terry was forced to drive 300 miles to where they were living to defend himself against it (which he did successfully). While he was there, though, his daughters refused to see or even speak to him. Their mother had poisoned them against Terry. As of this writing, he has resumed paying for their education, but they absolutely refuse all contact with him.

Clearly this is a sad and unusual situation, but it points out that the particulars of a divorce war often stem from one person's idiosyncrasies, fears, and foibles. Without judging Margaret, we can safely say that she made Terry's post-divorce life hell because she feared he might harm her or her children. That her fears are unfounded is irrelevant; they are what motivated her to seek an order of protection and turn Terry's daughters against him.

It's also worth noting that divorces can turn into wars at any point in the process. Some divorces start out friendly enough but quickly devolve into acrimony when one person does or says something "negative." I've found that it often doesn't take much to catalyze problems. For instance, a child reports that her dad had a "sleep-over" with another woman when the child was visiting. Or a father becomes furious when he discovers that his wife not only wants the main residence but the summer house that was handed down from his parents to him years ago. Or the catalyst may even be something innocuous, like a cross word or an inconsiderate comment exchanged on the phone.

In other instances, the war can erupt as soon as the papers are filed and someone is served. This is especially true when news about the divorce blindsides an individual and he feels betrayed, hurt, and angry. He may well explode verbally, make threats, and tell his attorney he wants to fight to the last penny for and over everything. In certain cases, though, this initial outburst represents the worst moment in the divorce process. Some people simply need to give voice to their anger. With time, they calm down and often are able to settle with their spouse without having to go to court or become involved in bitter exchanges.

I've also handled cases where wars were sporadic. They may have started off reasonably enough, then blown up, calmed down, and blown up again. In many instances, these up-and-down cases are the most difficult. When a blow-up is followed by a calm period, people often assume that the difficulty has been resolved and that the divorce will now proceed smoothly. It is incredibly frustrating, then, when the whole thing blows up again . . . and again . . . and again.

FIVE RULES FOR
MANAGING THE DIFFICULTY LEVEL

Obviously, you can't control what your spouse does. If your spouse is a maniac, you're in for a bumpy ride no matter what you do. Someone who is hell-bent on vengeance is going to try to make you suffer no matter how the person's actions impact you or your children. Nonetheless, you can follow some basic rules that may moderate or even avoid major difficulties. I'll elaborate on these rules throughout the book, but for now, they provide you with some basic principles that, if followed, can make your life during a divorce less unpleasant and the legal outcome more in keeping with what you'd hoped for.

1. Avoid rubbing salt in the wound.

No matter how much you despise your spouse, no matter how many ways you feel you've been wronged, don't make a bad situation worse by identifying your spouse's vulnerabilities when trying to reach a settlement. For instance, let's say the main arguments during your marriage revolved around your accusations that your wife was selfish. She would always become defensive when you made this accusation. Now, you're trying to reach a settlement about who gets what, and she tells you that she refuses to get a job, even though you've offered to provide support until she finds one. You respond, "That's just like you, always wanting things your own way. You can't get more selfish than that."

Whether your spouse is selfish is irrelevant, at least in terms of legal strategy. If your goal is to avoid a court battle and the high costs that go with it—and if you know that in addition to being selfish, your wife can be incredibly stubborn—then you want to avoid any accusations of selfishness. Be aware of your spouse's sensitivities and avoid inflaming them. It may gall you to do so, but keeping your spouse on an emotionally even keel generally results in a more positive outcome. Compromise is the essence of divorce negotiations, and if you say or do things that encourage your spouse to dig in and be inflexible, you're asking for a war. Always try to negotiate before you litigate, unless there's an emergency.

2. Think divorce first, romance second.

The most common factor that turns a normal divorce into an abnormally contentious one is bringing another man or woman into the mix. The situation is already potentially volatile, and all it takes is the mention that you have a new lover for your spouse to capitalize on that potential. You may feel the marriage is over, but your partner may not. It's also possible that both you and your spouse recognize intellectually that the marriage is no longer working, but emotionally that recognition hasn't sunk in. As a result, the emergence of a girlfriend or boyfriend is infuriating. Your spouse blames this individual for destroying the marriage, and it doesn't matter whether this person is to blame. Sometimes, people mention having a lover to rub the fact of it in their spouse's face. Other times the mention of a lover isn't designed to provoke, but the person in a new relationship has underestimated its impact. In still other situations, kids become aware of the new person and make his or her presence known to the other parent.

As a result, people may issue ridiculous demands ("You have a new girlfriend, but what have I got? The least you can do is let me have the house, the cars, and $50,000 a month"); they may tell their lawyer they want the divorce process to hurt their spouse as much as they've been hurt; or they may decide that their spouse isn't entitled to maintenance or custody or should see the kids only rarely because of his or her "treachery."

To avoid these situations, make a conscious effort to keep new relationships out of the conversations with your spouse. This is sometimes difficult to do, since people who were on the receiving end of the divorce news want to demonstrate to their spouse that someone out there finds them attractive and fun to be with even if they do not. I also am aware of people's tendency to show off what they feel is a new and improved love relationship. Don't give in to this tendency. At the very least, show discretion so that your kids aren't aware of this other relationship until after the divorce is concluded. The best decision is to wait until the divorce is done before exploring other relationships.

3. Agree with your spouse to put the children first.

Most people have good intentions and don't want to do any-thing to harm their children, but they inadvertently harm them when battles over property, visitation, custody, and the like spill over to affect the kids. Sometimes the kids overhear the fights. Sometimes one parent will falsely accuse a spouse of abuse or obtain orders of protection as a "legal tactic," and this can have a devastating impact on children. I have also seen the conse-quences of having children testify in court. When it's important for the judge to hear what children have to say, I often file a Mo-tion For In Camera Interview to occur in the judge's chambers, in which the judge speaks privately to the kids about their situa-tion. At least in my experience, no children have been "cross-examined" in these In Camera Interviews, which spare them the emotional trauma of this type of hostile questioning.

In some instances, however, lawyers will insist the children testify in court because they believe this will have the greatest effect on the court's decisions, or because their client insists on it. Cross-examining children about a parent's behavior—alcohol or drug abuse, physical or verbal abuse, neglect, or sexual conduct—can be psychologically scarring and throw them in the middle of the war between parents. This is especially true if the opposing attorney is not sensitive to these issues or feels he must discredit the children's testimony to protect his client.

Making a pact with your spouse to make decisions based on the best interests of the child can avoid many if not all of these negative events. Ideally, this means sitting down with your spouse at the very beginning of the divorce process and agreeing to forsake legal tactics and behaviors that might harm the kids. Re-alistically, it's not always easy to abide by these agreements, but having the discussion at the start increases the awareness that kids are vulnerable, and that both parents must bend over backwards to keep them as emotionally and psychologically safe and insulated from effects of the divorce as possible.

4. Bring in a therapist or mediator with expertise working with couples.

Yes, this adds some cost to the divorce, but it's money well spent, since therapists often can come up with ways to deal with difficult people that lawyers can't. When one or both people are angry, depressed, vengeful, or fearful, these emotions can turn a potentially simple, fast divorce into a complex, lengthy process. I'm not suggesting that therapists can work miracles and magically moderate the hatred one person feels for another, but sometimes they can foster understanding that takes the edge off that hatred. In one case, Phil was so furious with Nina at the start of the divorce proceeding that he couldn't even speak to her without making a threat. She had had an affair with his best friend, and he felt she had betrayed not only him but their kids. Phil wanted nothing more than to make her suffer, and as the only working parent with access to a significant amount of money, he could have done so. Instead, Phil's lawyer convinced him that he and Nina needed to talk to a therapist before beginning the legal work. Though their sessions were rough at first, they helped Phil understand how lonely Nina had been—Phil was a corporate law firm partner who frequently traveled abroad, and he had forced his wife to move with him two years ago from the city where all her relatives resided. Phil still didn't forgive Nina or want to try and work things out, but when the edge was removed from his anger, he was much more willing and able to work with her on a settlement that would be in the best interests of their children and be viewed as fair by both of them.

5. Avoid difficult attorneys.

I'll be discussing this last rule in greater detail in chapter 3, but for now, recognize that lawyers can turn good divorces into bad ones and bad divorces into nightmares. It's not just divorcing spouses who are difficult. Certain lawyers are intent on churning fees, and they can cleverly manipulate situations to their financial advantage. For instance, they can convince their clients that they will never receive their fair share of the property unless they go to court. They may insist on deposing scores of people. They may convince their clients it is necessary to secure testimony from eight different experts. They may also say or do things that increase the tensions between couples. I recall one case in which my client and I were meeting with the client's wife and her attorney. The meeting went reasonably well, and the couple was dealing with the issues like responsible adults. Nonetheless, the opposing attorney said to my client, "You know, you're going to lose custody." Not only was this statement untrue, but it made my client frantic and if I hadn't calmed him down, it would have resulted in a much more stressful and costly divorce.

In addition, some people are just asking for trouble. They fall for the myth that they have to find a take-no-prisoners attorney, someone who is ruthless and will use any tactic necessary to "win" the case. This myth, fueled by television and movies that depict the best lawyers in this manner, results in divorces where couples fight over both the little and big things and invariably end up in court and broke. In some instances, lawyers will subtly steer clients toward unethical practices (such as hiding money or filing false charges). When there is one difficult attorney, the odds are good that the divorce will be costly and unpleasant. When two difficult attorneys are involved, the odds are good that the process will be nightmarish.

I recognize that in the heat of a divorce, these five rules are easily ignored. When you feel like your wife is trying to destroy your life or your husband is trying to make you a pauper, you want to rub salt in your spouse's wound or find a lawyer who will fight dirty to ensure you get your fair share. As you'll discover, however, you can achieve your objectives by playing within these rules. In the following chapters, you'll find out how to do so.

CHAPTER THREE

How to Find
the Best Lawyer for
the Worst Cases

Some attorneys are perfectly competent when it comes to uncontested divorces, but when the divorces become wars, they may be out of their depth. Many lawyers have never handled a case in which one spouse falsely accused the other of abusing the kids as a negotiating ploy or where sophisticated financial scams were involved. In fact, some divorce lawyers rarely if ever have litigated in court, having always managed to settle relatively simple cases. Dealing with ugly fights over custody or visitation and abuse charges may be beyond their abilities. If they try to fake it, they do their clients a great disservice. They may advise clients to settle when they should go to trial or advise them to go to trial when they should settle. They may fail to recognize that a forensic accountant is needed to find hidden monies or that an expert needs to be brought in to value complex assets and help ensure a fair split is achieved. They may try to act the part of a blustering, aggressive attorney and put on a dog-and-pony show to camouflage their lack of skill, a performance that drives legal costs through the roof and provokes their client's spouse to demand sole custody when he might have been willing to agree to joint custody or even visitation.

No matter where you live, the odds are that within your geographical area exist a number of highly competent attorneys who will represent you well no matter how difficult your divorce might be. The bad news is that there are probably a much greater number of lawyers who shouldn't be allowed near a difficult divorce. Unfortunately, both types of lawyers look alike to the untrained eye. Therefore, I'd like to help you differentiate between the two and maximize the value of the highly competent ones. The first thing you're going to need to know is what to do when you realize you have to find a lawyer.

INITIAL STEPS: THE SEARCH FOR A
SAVVY DIVORCE ATTORNEY

When people realize they need to hire a lawyer, they tend to do one of four things:

- Ask a friend who has been divorced for the name of his lawyer.

- Call a lawyer who has handled other legal matters for them and ask if she does divorce work.

- Hire a lawyer who is also a trusted friend.

- Look on the Web or in the yellow pages for lawyers in their area who advertise that they handle divorces.

All four of these tactics are fraught with peril if you become caught up in a divorce war. For instance, your friend may tell you that her lawyer was relatively inexpensive and helped her expedite her divorce quickly and with little emotional pain. This lawyer, however, may have little or no experience with complex or contested divorces, and you may discover that her advice during the divorce process is well-meaning but based on false assumptions (such as that it's always better to reach a settlement than to go to court). It's also possible that an inexpensive, inexperienced attorney may completely miss the signals that your spouse is scheming to hide assets or is planning to drain your joint accounts, liquidate investments, and leave the country with the children.

Similarly, people frequently believe that their "generalist" lawyer is as capable of handling their divorce as he was of handling their real-estate closing or parking tickets. This may be true if the divorce is simple, but general-practice lawyers may find themselves out of their depth when their clients' spouses are devious or irrational or when a case becomes a complex financial chess match. Nonetheless, they may assure you that they've handled many divorces before and that they would be glad to take yours on.

The third possibility—hiring a lawyer who is also a friend—may seem to make sense on the surface, since you know your friendship ensures this lawyer will be honest with you and do his best. However, even if your friend is an experienced divorce attorney who has handled ugly cases, his friendship will probably diminish his effectiveness. Divorce wars can become highly emotional; you may tell your attorney in a fit of anger that you don't care what it costs, you're going to make your spouse pay for what he's doing to you. Will your friend and lawyer be capable of taking a step back and assessing the situation objectively? Or will he become caught up in your possibly justifiable anger and vow to you that *"we're* going to make him pay!"?

The problem with searching for a lawyer on the Web or in the phone book is obvious: You don't know what you're getting. While Web sites or ads in the yellow pages may do a good job of convincing you that someone is the best divorce lawyer around, they may not present a complete story of a given lawyer's or firm's competence regarding family law matters. No matter how many endorsements lawyers list on their site or how many legal organizations to which they belong or how convincing the verbiage is about their family law expertise, they may never have handled a tough case; they may never have dealt with a spouse who vows to destroy visitation with the kids unless the client hands over an unfair percentage of the marital property.

Be aware, too, that in some states there is no such thing as a family or matrimonial law specialist. In Illinois, for instance, the state's supreme court does not recognize certification of specialization in this practice of law. While some people claim to be certified as a specialist in this area and have business cards or ads that make this claim, they may be acting in a deceptive manner in states where such conduct is a violation of the Rules of Professional Conduct. Specialists certainly exist in some states, but be wary of attorneys who state or imply this is an "official" designation in a state with no specialty designation.

So how do you find a savvy divorce attorney? The best thing you can do is talk to people you know who have gone through difficult divorces and ask them about their lawyers. Were they satisfied with them? Do they believe they demonstrated skill and knowledge in helping them navigate tricky or complicated passages in the process? Ideally, you want to discover lawyers who have handled cases similar to what you expect yours to be. If you're anticipating a financial nightmare, for instance, you want to find someone who has worked closely with forensic accountants in the past. One caveat about this search: Talk to people who have gone through divorces in the last few years. You may find someone who raves about how great her divorce lawyer was, but if the case took place fifteen years ago, it's possible that the lawyer has lost his drive or is no longer on the cutting edge.

If you know or have other attorneys who aren't family law experts, it's fine to tap them for the names of specialists. Remember, though, to emphasize that you anticipate a difficult divorce and that you want the names of lawyers who they feel are savvy about these types of cases.

Another strategy to consider is perusing local newspapers and magazines online for attorneys who have been involved in high-profile and complex cases. Periodically, dramatic custody cases make news, as do divorces involving people with a high net worth. You may also read an insightful op ed piece by a divorce lawyer or a profile of this individual. While it's difficult to know for sure whether these individuals are as good as their publicity suggests, you at least know that they've been involved in complex cases or that someone (a newspaper editor) believes they are savvy.

Use this research and your networking to create a list of potential candidates to represent you. Ideally, you'll list at least three lawyers who seem to have the qualifications you require. You may find, however, that your initial list is quite long, especially if you live in a large city. In this case, you're going to need a way to prune it to about three names.

SEPARATING THE WHEAT FROM THE CHAFF

Before you visit any of the lawyers on your list, you can do a number of things to eliminate those who are probably not right for you. Specifically:

- **Call or e-mail (or write) each lawyer on your list and ask if you can talk to a client (or clients) they've successfully represented with a case similar to your own after your initial consultation.** In other words, if you want joint custody and your spouse refuses to grant it to you, talk to someone who was in a similar predicament. You're looking for an attorney who has handled similar cases and is willing to let you talk to the clients in those cases.

- **Ask the attorneys on the list what percentage of their cases settle out of court.** What you're looking for is a percentage of between 80 and 90 percent. If it is significantly less than 70 percent, the attorney is probably overly fond of going to trial—perhaps because she is interested in the additional billing that results. If it's more than 90 percent, the attorney may lack both the gumption and trial experience you'll need if your difficult case proves impossible to settle.

- **Cross off the list any attorneys who immediately guarantee you any specific result.** In difficult cases, especially, it is impossible to guarantee anything. Nonetheless, you'll probably encounter someone who tells you something like "Your case is a slam dunk. I don't see any way that you'll have to pay her *x* number of dollars. And I'm sure I can get you the visitation schedule you want." On the other hand, if an attorney is honest and says that because the case may be difficult, it is impossible to predict with absolute certainty the outcome, but he'll handcraft a strategy for you and do everything possible to achieve the outcome you desire, circle that name.

- **Ask the attorney what percentage of her practice involves family law (or look at her Web site).** If the family law portion is 50 percent or less, eliminate that lawyer from consideration. Ideally, you want a lawyer who spends all her time on divorce-related matters. You want someone who has seen and done it all. You don't want her to be thrown when your spouse does something crazy or your spouse's lawyer springs a surprise. If an attorney has been handling only family law cases for seven to ten years, the odds are she's had her share of difficult ones and will be prepared for whatever your case involves.

THE INITIAL INTERVIEW

When you walk through an attorney's door for the first time, you need to be an active participant in the interview. I emphasize this point because too many people enter an office and are passive recipients of whatever it is the lawyer has to say. By engaging in a dialogue rather than listening to a monologue (often a canned speech the lawyer gives to all his prospective clients), you can be a better judge if this particular attorney is capable of handling a difficult divorce.

Start off making sure you fill in the blanks left from your phone conversation regarding the earlier five points. You may not have had time to cover everything, so be sure to find out what percentage of the lawyer's practice is family law, whether he begins the conversations by guaranteeing results, and so on.

Next, the attorney will probably talk a bit about what he does, his philosophy, and his experience. While much of this will be innocuous, watch for the following red flags:

- **Any articulated biases regarding divorce.** Some attorneys believe that children are best off with their mothers regardless of the situation. Others are convinced that being highly aggressive and confrontational yields the best results when a client's spouse is being obstinate. These one-size-fits-all ideas are especially counterproductive in difficult divorces. To paraphrase Tolstoy's opening line of *Anna Karenina,* "Each difficult divorce is difficult in its own way." You want your lawyer to be flexible and situational, and if he has fixed ideas or biases about how all divorces should proceed, you don't want this lawyer handling your case.

- **Premature pronouncements about strategy or outcomes.** Your case may be complicated or involve serious disagreements on big issues, but you don't want a lawyer who, upon hearing your summary, says to you, "You're doomed" (or words to that effect). To handle potentially ugly cases effectively, lawyers need to be open-minded and creative about both strategy and potential outcomes. If they're convinced you are going to lose your kids, your house, your savings, and so on, this attitude likely will become a self-fulfilling prophecy. Similarly, lawyers who are falsely optimistic won't be able to deal with the harsh realities of a combative spouse or an opposing lawyer who uses underhanded tactics. When these lawyers find that their optimistic forecast was way off, they may advise giving in prematurely.

- **An inability to suggest a preliminary strategy.** This is a good litmus test to determine whether a lawyer has the experience and savvy necessary to handle a messy, contested case. You want someone who can hear the summary of your situation and come up with an initial plan of action. Sometimes, difficult cases can be made far less difficult by adopting the right approach early on. Rather than antagonize an angry spouse, there are ways to defuse a potentially explosive situation. Rather than allow someone to manipulate the family finances in a way that will give him an unfair share, a good lawyer can often spot this scenario and take steps to nip it in the bud. While no lawyer can immediately tell you exactly what to do from a brief summary, you should expect some concrete ideas. If you don't get any—if the attorney refuses to give you a sense of how he might handle this difficult case—this probably isn't the right advocate for you.

Besides being alert for these red flags, you should go into the initial interview armed with the following questions designed to assess the lawyer's ability to handle what could be a complex, emotional case that eventually might only be resolved in court.

Are you familiar with the attitudes and inclinations of local judges?

If you can't reach a settlement, you're going to end up in court, and your attorney's ability to "read" a judge and present a case that is likely to sway a particular judge in your favor is key. Judges have a great deal of discretion in divorce cases, and it helps tremendously if your attorney demonstrates that he knows which judge is intolerant of any type of financial manipulation and which judge is a strong believer in joint custody. Some judges are gender neutral, some are pro-male, and some are pro-female. You lawyer should know in which direction a judge may lean.

Do you know and recommend therapists to facilitate the divorce process, especially when there is a lot of anger on the part of one or both parties?

As mentioned before, good therapists can help both parties in a divorce learn to manage their anger, both for their own benefit and that of their children. Some attorneys don't like to involve therapists, feeling that they can "muddy" the legal waters and that their fees decrease the money available to pay legal fees. You want to find a lawyer who recognizes the value of therapists and has at least one or two with whom he has worked extensively and who he knows are skilled at helping people deal rationally and objectively with their turbulent, divorce-related emotions.

Can you describe the range of experts you have worked with in the past?

Ideally, an attorney will mention forensic accountants, real-estate appraisers, employee benefits specialists (actuaries), CLUs (chartered life underwriters), pediatric psychiatrists, financial planners, and others. This doesn't mean that you're going to require all of these experts in your case, only that your attorney has experience and contacts in whatever area proves difficult in your divorce.

Can you cite at least a few different ways you've resolved custody disputes?

Custody conflicts are among the most common reasons divorces become difficult. If your attorney can cite only one strategy to resolve custody disputes, than she is probably a bad choice. A lawyer experienced in this area has found all sorts of different ways to break custody deadlocks so that both parties are satisfied. They may involve using a financial advantage to protect the best interests of the children. It may mean promising a temporary period of judicial supervision in order to prove a parent will be responsible in a custodial role, or using case law to make a convincing argument to a judge that his client's custody request has substantial merit.

Are you available on a 24/7 basis?

In a major divorce fight, you need your attorney to be available to you around the clock. Crises are not uncommon. Your spouse may be threatening to kidnap the children, he may physically abuse you in the middle of the night, or you may be checking your bank statement over the weekend and realize funds are mysteriously disappearing from an account. While you don't want to abuse this 24-hour availability, your lawyer should understand that in a difficult case, emergencies and surprises can happen at any time and that time is of the essence in critical attorney-client communications to limit the damage.

What was the most difficult divorce case you've ever handled, and what was the outcome?

Lawyers generally are not shy about telling war stories, and they should not have any problem coming up with one that illustrates their ability to manage a case that threatens to blow up. If all a lawyer can tell you is that he helped reduce a child-care payment by a small amount or ensured that a spouse received a percentage of a retirement benefit she wasn't sure she would get, then it's clear that the lawyer hasn't handled many tough cases. What you want to hear is the story of how the lawyer managed to gain joint custody for a dad even though the mom was dead set against it at the beginning and legal precedent was in her favor. Or you want to hear about how an attorney made sure a mom was able to delay returning to the workforce in order to be at home with her young children despite the inclination of judges to order women back to work in similar situations.

Do you have a good private investigator on retainer or with whom you work regularly?

Warlike divorce cases can go in all sorts of strange directions, and sometimes nuggets of information that can make a difference for a client aren't readily available. For instance, I've had cases where my client's spouse seemed like an upstanding citizen, but my client insisted she was using drugs in front of the children or frequently fell into alcoholic rages and threatened them. These people, however, were smart enough to be discreet about such behaviors and so didn't have an arrest record or adult witnesses to the behaviors.

Private investigators have tools and techniques to gather evidence that can be obtained in no other way. I've had investigators who found critical pieces of evidence by sifting through the trash or by following an individual for weeks. They learn where these spouses buy their liquor and how much they buy; they are able to figure out who is supplying them with dope; they know if they're working with a shady financial person who has a reputation for hiding assets during divorces. While this evidence is not always admissible in court, it can be sufficient to motivate the other party to compromise and strike a fair settlement.

Not all private investigators are good, however, and we'll discuss how to use a good one productively later on. For now, just make sure the attorneys you interview have investigators they rely on and that they are licensed as private detectives.

Finally, when you've assessed attorneys on all these points and still aren't sure whom to hire, trust your impressions. Ask yourself how an attorney sounded when you talked. Was he bored and disinterested? Did he seem wary of your case based on the difficulties you touched upon? Did he keep interrupting your conversation to take other calls or talk to someone else in his office? While it's not always easy to assess someone based on a brief conversation, you often can pick up cues suggesting a lawyer isn't interested in handling a complex or dicey case.

THE MOST COMMON MISTAKES

Despite taking all the precautions above, you may still fall into the traps that plague many people going through divorce battles. If you're angry, depressed, or not thinking clearly for any reason, you may choose an attorney based more on style than substance, or based on what you think and hope he can do rather than his true capabilities. To prevent that from happening, consider three common (but easily preventable) mistakes people make when hiring lawyers to handle ugly divorces:

Hire the first lawyer they interview

Many times, people pour out their heart to the first lawyer they talk to. They have so much sadness or other powerful emotions coursing through them that when a lawyer questions them about why they're getting divorced, they naturally go beyond the facts of the case to issues of betrayal, vengeance, guilt, and so on. This lawyer may be the first one to whom they've unburdened themselves, and as a result, they feel a connection with her.

Therefore, it seems logical to hire her. In many instances, however, this decision is more emotional than logical. This lawyer may seem to understand you and your particular difficulties with your spouse, but she may not be qualified to handle those difficulties from a legal perspective. It is far better to interview at least two additional attorneys and then evaluate all three based on the criteria we've already established.

Choose an attorney primarily because of his aggressiveness

You know your spouse is going to be difficult about the divorce. You're convinced he's going to fight tooth and nail over every little thing. You suspect that he's willing to file false charges against you in order to punish you for your infidelity. Because of this, you're sure you're in for a fight, and therefore you reason that you should hire an attorney who is clearly a willing combatant. As a result, when a lawyer presents himself as a "shark" who "guarantees" he's going to go after your spouse with everything he's got, you think, "This is the lawyer for me."

Not necessarily. Overly aggressive lawyers are spoiling for a fight. They may escalate tensions between you and your spouse, resulting in a drawn-out and expensive period of depositions, scores of expert witnesses, and a full-blown trial. While it's important to have an attorney who knows how to push hard for what you believe is fair, you don't want one who knows only one way to handle a divorce.

Select a lawyer because she emphasizes her ability to achieve consensus and reach settlements

Similarly, the attorney who presents herself as conciliatory and accommodating may not be appropriate in certain difficult circumstances. When the other side is making outrageous demands and refuses to move an inch, you want your lawyer to play hardball. If your spouse is acting irrationally, it may be impossible to reach consensus on anything. If your spouse is a threat to you or your children or involved in illegal activities, you want your lawyer to be tough and proactive. In short, you want an attorney who is capable of being both consensus-driven and aggressive, but who doesn't lock into either mode prematurely.

Hire an attorney because he works at one of the city's biggest law firms that lacks family law practitioners

People are impressed by the names of law firms they know. When they anticipate a difficult divorce, they reason that if they can hire someone from a large and clout-heavy firm, they will have access to valuable resources. They assume an attorney attached to a top firm will inspire fear in their spouse, will have good connections with judges, and is top-of-his-class smart or he wouldn't have been hired by the firm in the first place.

Actually, current or previous employment at a top firm means nothing, at least from a family law perspective. The best divorce lawyers are the ones who have the experience and the instinct— the experience handling a wide variety of tough cases and the instinct to know what to do during critical moments as the case unfolds. Many years ago, I hired a trial lawyer from a top firm because he had an excellent record as a litigator (though not in family law). Still, he was smart and quick-witted and knew the law, and I figured he would make a successful transition to divorce law. Not only was I wrong, but this attorney didn't last even two months and almost had a nervous breakdown. He lacked the emotional stamina divorce lawyers need, and he panicked when he had to recommend a course of action in a difficult case, since he lacked the instinct to know what to do.

Pick an attorney with an oversized ego

The rationale is similar to that for choosing a highly aggressive lawyer. You want someone who exudes confidence, who can diminish your fears that you'll lose custody or that your spouse will get away with financial murder when property is divided. The attorney who tells you that he is the best, that he has won more divorce fights than anyone in town, is enormously appealing.

The problem is that egotistic divorce lawyers can mess up even simple divorce cases. During a volatile process, there may be times when they must swallow their pride and admit they made a mistake with their earlier assertion that no expert witnesses were necessary and that it's time to change tactics. Or they may have to be gracious and maintain their cool even if the opposing attorney is insulting. In certain situations, too, they may have to discount negative client behaviors. I have observed people going through a divorce who take out their anger on their lawyer in the court hallways; they accuse the attorney of everything from laziness to overaggressiveness and say something to the effect of "If you had done X, I wouldn't be facing the loss of my job." The egotistical lawyer may think, "Screw him. I'm through working my tail off for him; I'm just going to go through the motions."

I've also seen egotistical lawyers, upset with their clients, who have taken out their anger in legally counterproductive ways. For example, the opposing attorney in one case was representing my client's wife, and he was furious with her because some of her actions had weakened her motion for sole custody; he felt these actions had damaged the case. At one point, this attorney and I were called in to meet with the judge in his chambers, and the lawyer made a number of disparaging remarks about his own client. My client was awarded sole custody, in no small part because this lawyer felt compelled to bad-mouth his client's character and give the judge a reason to rule for custody in my client's favor.

HOW TO MAXIMIZE
YOUR ATTORNEY'S EFFECTIVENESS

Whether your relationship with a divorce attorney lasts for weeks, months, or years, you can do a number of things to increase the odds that she'll do a good job, no matter how problematic your divorce might be. The following are Lawyer Relationship Rules that can make the difference between your attorney being 75 percent effective versus 100 percent:

Rule #1: Be completely honest and forthcoming about any divorce-related issue.

Just as you want to tell your doctor everything about your medical condition so he can suggest the best possible treatment plan, you want to give your lawyer as much information as possible to help you. Recognize, however, that you may not want to tell your lawyer everything because you're embarrassed or you believe the lawyer will think you're paranoid or nuts. For instance, you may not want to reveal that your spouse didn't have just one affair but scores of them. If you're a man, you may not want anyone to know that your wife routinely hit you with pots and kicked you whenever she was angry. It's also possible that you want to protect your spouse and don't feel comfortable telling a relative stranger about her horrible behavior.

You must get past these concerns if you want your attorney to do a good job. I know of one client who lost his fight for joint custody in large part because he failed to inform his lawyer that his spouse had been taking medication for depression and anxiety for years, and that sometimes when she was off her meds she was derelict in her duties as a parent. This individual did not tell his attorney about her problems—or how he'd had to take over sole parenting responsibilities for extended periods of time—because she had been doing well for the past year and he did not want to embarrass her or cause her unnecessary pain. He claimed she was a good mom and avoided discussing this sensitive issue. His wife, however, was not similarly considerate of his feelings, using his extensive work travel schedule and past problems with drinking (he had been sober for five years prior to the divorce) as reasons he should not be granted joint custody. This man didn't realize that had he been completely forthcoming about this issue, his lawyer might have found a way to use the information in a manner that would not have embarrassed his wife.

Rule #2: Keep your attorney informed of any developments that might have a bearing on the case.

As I stated earlier, you should have access to your attorney 24/7. If something happens that concerns you or that you believe might negatively impact your divorce objectives, tell her immediately. If your spouse is manipulative, threatening, or abusive, this is especially important, since he may pull some stunt that can affect you or your children adversely. If you suspect your spouse is up to no good, share your suspicions immediately. His behavior may mean nothing, or it may be part of a strategy designed to take away your children, your money, your property, or your sanity.

A few years ago, I received a call from a client in the early evening. He apologized for bothering me and said he felt stupid calling and that his concern was probably trivial, but his wife had asked him if he would get a hotel room just for the night. She said that she loved him, but she needed some time alone with the kids. He said he was going to do what she requested.

I told him that he should not do it. They were in the middle of the divorce process, and from other information he had supplied me about his wife, it seemed clear that this was a ploy to get him out of the house and change the locks—a ploy that may well have been suggested to her by her attorney, since many other custodial parents have used it. I warned my client that when he came home the next day, he would find that the locks had been changed. When he pounded on the door and his wife refused to let him in, she would call the police and tell them that he had moved out and was living in a hotel. She would tell them to ask him where he'd stayed the previous night and if he had keys to the house. Then, her attorney would go to court immediately and file and argue a Motion to Maintain the Status Quo and Exclusive Possession. In many instances, judges grant these motions because they want to avoid disrupting children's lives as much as possible, and the reasoning is that if their father isn't living at home now, why create a disruption by allowing him to move back in.

The bottom line: Tell your attorney about any unusual or suspicious actions or requests involving your spouse.

Rule #3: Don't expect your lawyer to become your friend.

Like therapists, lawyers often are privy to intimate details of their clients' lives, and sharing of this information often creates an emotional bond, at least from the clients' perspective. However, lawyers, like therapists, are no good to their clients if they lose their objectivity. If they're buddies with their clients, they often get caught up in the emotion of the divorce and act out of anger or solidarity rather than based on objective analysis. They may pursue a strategy designed to get a client sole custody because they feel it's the right thing and it's what the client wants most of all, ignoring the fact that the situation makes this objective unreachable and that its pursuit will result in enormous legal and emotional costs.

In some instances, lawyers become so caught up in their clients' situations that they conspire to commit crimes to gain favorable settlements. They may suggest that a client hide money in an offshore account or conspire with her to entrap her spouse—provoking him to strike her, for instance. A client may call his friend the lawyer and talk about all the horrible things his spouse is contemplating, and the lawyer will naturally be outraged by her fiendish behavior. The client may say, "She's going to accuse me of sexually abusing the kids, even though she knows that has never happened and never will happen." "Well," the lawyer might respond, sympathetic to his friend's plight, "we could preempt that move by accusing her of neglecting her kids first." Not only is this ethically wrong and illegal, but it turns the children into pawns and ultimately victimizes them.

You should endeavor to maintain a trusting but professional relationship with your lawyer. Your lawyer's objectivity is tremendously valuable to you, and you should do nothing to detract from it.

Rule #4: If you suspect your lawyer is not doing a competent job, obtain a second opinion.

I list this final rule with a bit of hesitation. During the course of a difficult divorce, ups and downs are inevitable. Rulings go against clients that shouldn't and spouses go ballistic without any provocation. In these situations, lawyers are easy targets for their clients' ire. As a client in a difficult divorce, you need to be prepared for a volatile process and recognize that if your spouse is vengeful, manipulative, and abusive, you're going to go through some tough times before the divorce is final. For this reason, you need to give your attorney the benefit of the doubt and believe that if you did a good job in choosing him, he probably will do a good job for you.

That written, I should add that you are perfectly within your rights to assess his performance, and you should do so. If you don't understand why he took a particular action or did something that seems contrary to your wishes, you should question him. If you're not satisfied with his response, you should seek a second opinion.

To do so, though, you're going to need your case file. To this end, you should always have a copy of all the documents pertaining to your case that you can then share with another lawyer. Without examining all these documents, it's difficult for another lawyer to give you an informed second opinion. With them, he should be able to tell you if your lawyer has made major mistakes and if finding a new attorney is warranted.

Besides these four rules, I would encourage you to depend on your lawyer to keep her head when all those around her are losing theirs. If your divorce proves to be combative and stressful, you want your attorney to be a port in the storm. You need to depend on your attorney to analyze situations logically when everyone else is being emotional; you need her to suggest options when everyone is insisting there is only way to resolve matters. Don't expect your attorney to become as enraged as you are; you don't want her to lose her objectivity. Don't be disappointed if she doesn't start cursing your spouse the way you've cursed him. Instead, value your lawyer's objectivity and calm, since it may provide you with a way to come to terms with a spouse who is anything but.

CHAPTER FOUR

Know Your Enemy:
Identifying Traits and Tendencies
That Can Push You into Divorce Hell

It takes two to tango. In certain instances, divorce battles are a result of two good people at their worst dug in on certain issues, with neither one willing to give an inch. In other instances, you're going through a divorce war because your spouse is impossible. In this chapter, we will discuss the latter scenario—and then introduce the terminology of "jerk." After you've found a lawyer who has extensive experience dealing with ugly divorces, you need to talk with your lawyer about the particular way in which your spouse will act and react throughout the process.

When it comes to divorce, difficult people come in all shapes and sizes. Some of them are born and some are made by the divorce process, but in either case you need to identify the type that is hounding you.

These individuals behave in different ways during this difficult time, and if you understand the type you're dealing with, you will be better able to achieve your divorce goals. As you'll see, I've divided the types into three broad categories: money, abuse, and vengeance. You should also be aware, though, that within each category exist the subtypes of temporary and permanent jerks.

A temporary jerk's bad behavior is a result of the crumbling marriage and the divorce process rather than intrinsic meanness. It's important to understand the distinction, as temporary jerks sometimes can be reasoned with. They may respond to best-interest-of-the-child appeals or back off from extreme positions during settlement negotiations. Permanent jerks, on the other hand, are not particularly nice people and need to be approached with caution during negotiations and in court.

Later, I'll provide you with a tool to differentiate temporary from permanent jerks, which is not always easy to accomplish on your own. In fact, many men and women have trouble confronting the reality of their divorcing spouse's bad traits.

If you're like most people, you've spent the years prior to your divorce in denial about who your spouse really is. Rather than seeking to understand your partner's character and flaws, you've been overlooking them in order to maintain the peaceful coexistence that has kept the marriage intact.

But now that the marriage is ending, you must face reality. Only by knowing your spouse's true character can you predict what this person is likely to do during the divorce process and in its wake. By doing so, you can protect yourself and your children from financial chicanery, physical and emotional abuse, and vengeance-seeking tactics.

THE MONEY OBSESSIVE

Once you or your partner has decided to get divorced, one of the first things you have to consider is money. There's nothing like money to bring out the worst in people. Divorce often magnifies a person's natural tendencies, so if your spouse is someone who has been financially generous and has the resources to take care of your family, chances are you're in luck; those traits are likely to remain in evidence or even intensify. People often use money to compensate for the guilt brought on by the divorce or an affair, so a generous person may become more generous than ever.

If, however, your marriage has been marked by money fights—accusations of being a skinflint or a spendthrift, arguments over how to manage your money—don't expect things to change for the better. Divorce is one of the leading causes of money problems—suddenly there's another household to support on the same income—so anticipate that the financial tensions will escalate.

To determine whether your spouse is a money obsessive—if he or she is likely to use money as a weapon against you—answer the following questions:

- Did your spouse manifest extreme money behaviors during your marriage, such as excessive spending, irrational fear of spending, or chaotic money management habits?

- Did you and your spouse engage in frequent fights about money?

- Is your spouse the breadwinner while you are the stay-at-home parent?

- Did you notice your spouse making a number of mysterious banking transactions or conferring with a financial advisor before announcing that he wanted a divorce?

- Did your spouse suggest you'd end up in the poor house when you announced you wanted a divorce?

- During the initial stages of the divorce process, did your spouse claim to have much less money than you know she really possessed?

- Has your spouse threatened to stop working rather than pay the money you need to survive?

- Has your spouse refused to settle, and is he insisting on going to trial because he wants to drive up your legal fees? (He may have told you this is his intent, or you may suspect it.)

- Does your spouse claim to have relatively little money while living a lavish lifestyle during the divorce process?

If you record more than five yes answers, your spouse is probably a money obsessive.

To combat your spouse's worst tendencies, the following steps are strongly recommended:

1. **Obtain a court order that prohibits the other side from disposing of all assets and completely draining your accounts.** A restraining order or injunction may do the job in many cases because if the other side violates it, the client and sometimes the attorney can be found in contempt of court

and incarcerated. Be aware, however, that if you are dealing with an extreme money obsessive a legal action such as this one can drive him over the edge. I know more than one person who preferred going to jail to giving one additional penny to his spouse. I also know people who have disappeared when court action was threatened, and others who have resorted to violence.

You and your attorney need to assess the risk, but chances are you are dealing with a garden-variety money obsessive who won't take these drastic measures. In these instances, don't make the mistake many divorce lawyers make: threatening or serving your spouse with a standard Motion for a Temporary Restraining Order. This gives him time to hide as much money as possible after being threatened or notified to appear in court. It may be to your benefit to instead consider seeking an emergency ex parte action—a restraining order or injunction obtained without notifying your spouse or his attorney. If the ex parte action is handled correctly, they won't even know you're in court, so they won't be motivated to respond with a preemptive strike such as transferring money out of the country or draining all your accounts prior to the court date.

2. **Enjoin other parties who have access to the funds.** Even if you have a restraining order or injunction against your spouse, it may have no effect on the financial entities— banks, brokerage houses, financial advisors, and the like— that actually have their hands on your money. All the other side has to do is instruct the bank or the broker to transfer funds to another institution, and the money in effect may be gone and you may never be able to locate it. On the other hand, any reputable bank or brokerage firm joined as a

third party to the divorce likely will cooperate with a restraining order or injunction that prohibits it from transferring funds from the account. This means the funds likely will be protected and you will know where they are.

3. **Transfer funds to an institution.** To accomplish this, you should obtain a court order transferring the funds to a bank and setting up a trust account at that bank naming your attorney or both of the opposing attorneys as trustee(s), whereby only the trustee(s) can release the funds. However, the court must state the funds cannot be released by the trustees without a subsequent court order approving the recipient and amount of any distribution. Be sure to serve notice of this court order on the bank and have proof of their receipt of it.

4. **Use the Notice for Deposition as a tool to get the right financial documents from your spouse.** Preparation for your spouse's deposition begins with the Notice for Deposition, which most attorneys complete as a routine fill-in-the-blank form without a rider. This is a big mistake. The notice never should be completed without attaching a handcrafted rider that requests every single document you want the other side to produce at the deposition. Many lawyers don't attach this, but they're missing an enormous opportunity, because without such a rider the other side won't be compelled to bring important documents to the deposition that you could use in questioning the witness. While your attorney can file a Notice to Produce, requesting all kinds of documents after the deposition, it will be too late to prevent assets from disappearing. This may also prompt the other side to pull the oldest trick in

the book: altering, concealing, or "losing" all-important paperwork. By adding the rider to the deposition notice, you greatly increase the chances that you will leave the deposition with the documents and information you need to help prevent assets from being permanently hidden. These documents may also aid you in examining the witness.

5. **Obtain all documentation for every account in the bank as part of your deposition request.** Many lawyers fail to find all the money obsessive's bank accounts because the obsessive can use various tricks to hide accounts. Your spouse may have accounts in her maiden name or she may be listed as the beneficiary on an account in someone else's name when the money actually belongs to her. Or she may even hide money in a friend's or relative's account. Go through every signature card and look for authorized signers; these signers may be hiding your spouse's funds. When you review every single statement and cancelled check and see a mysterious check for $10,000 deposited in an account you know nothing about, get a copy of the check—both front and back—so you can see where it was cashed or deposited. Then you can subpoena that bank and continue pursuing the paper trail. And don't overlook safety deposit boxes, which often contain clues to lots of important information, and sometimes cash. You need an injunction to freeze the contents, which must specify a date and time to inspect the box, and you need an official from the bank and your attorney to witness the inspection. Otherwise, you may be inspecting an empty box.

By and large, these steps represent a small amount of labor, at least relative to the huge problems they can prevent. You should be aware that there are new and improved money-hiding strategies being invented every day. Therefore, if you suspect your spouse of hiding money, these five steps can save you a bundle. I recently had a case where the husband had set up more than thirty separate corporations throughout the country, so I had to serve each corporation's registered agent individually to begin the process of tracing funds and piercing corporate veils. This man also had offshore trusts, which are very difficult to penetrate. By persistently tracking the paper trail, we were able to get much of the information we needed. As a result, the other side ended up in a panic and agreed to settle the case.

Unfortunately, this case involved creditor protection trusts, vehicles designed specifically to thwart penetration by creditors. These are very useful for shielding funds. But the thing to remember is that no financial vehicle is completely impenetrable, and if your lawyer works hard enough and hires the right experts—and smart enough—you may obtain the information you need and protect yourself from a spouse who would pick your pocket.

Here's another tip: You may not be able to get your spouse to be reasonable about money, but you may be able to convince her lawyer to apply some pressure. If you suspect your spouse is doing something illegal, such as wrongfully hiding funds, and you have evidence to prove it (or you believe you can obtain this evidence), your attorney may want to have a serious conversation with your opponent's attorney about this.

Sometimes, too, the other attorney may be motivated to act because of her own financial concerns or her professional liability. I once was up against a very difficult woman who initiated divorce proceedings against my client. She had managed to wrest control of the marital accounts, which were substantial, but she was refusing to pay my client his fair share and contribute to my fees. I discussed the situation with her lawyer, who said, "I don't really care if she won't pay him or you, because she paid me, and she has the money." In response, I filed a Petition to Disgorge the other attorney of half the fee she was paid in the interest of fairness and leveling the playing field. I also initiated a civil contempt proceeding for support owed against the other party, which could have resulted in her serving jail time. This immediately had the effect of making the attorney and her client more reasonable. Soon my client parted with a significant portion of the money at her counsel's direction.

One final tip about finding funds a money obsessive may be hiding: Consider using a forensic accountant. These accountants specialize in detecting fraud, and if you have strong suspicions about your spouse, there is a significant amount of money involved, and he is financially sophisticated, a highly skilled forensic accountant may be your best bet.

Forensic accountants are expensive, but they're also valuable in assisting your attorney in getting the information you need and identifying fraud. If your side can prove fraud, you probably can force the other side to pay the cost of the forensic accountant, too, if the court has not already ordered the other side to pay in advance.

THE ABUSER

Divorce can bring out the latent abuser in both men and women. The tremendous anger that the process creates can cause people to say and do harmful things to each other and even to their children. Physical abuse, obviously, is usually the more serious threat, but verbal abuse is more common and also can be very destructive. You need to be alert for both, as any kind of abuse can affect your physical and emotional well-being. Abuse in any form is likely to be considered domestic violence, particularly from a legal perspective. Some people, faced with a psychologically astute abuser, will agree to things they never should agree to, just to try to diminish the abuse. Others feel so guilty as a result of their spouse's accusations that they voluntarily make concessions they should never have made. Some individuals leave the divorce with a fair settlement but with their self-esteem, their relationships with their children, and even their children's emotional health destroyed by an abusive spouse.

Certainly you don't need this book to determine whether your spouse is abusing you or your children, but you do need to learn how to respond to this abuse from a legal standpoint to avoid becoming a victim. Here are some questions you need to ask yourself to fashion an effective legal response:

1. Did the verbal abuse start at the time you or your spouse filed for divorce, or has it escalated since that time?

If your spouse was not abusive before the divorce process began, the change may signal a conscious decision to be abusive. She may be using verbal attacks to gain psychological leverage in the case. I know of a woman who constantly emasculated her husband, berating him relentlessly about being a lousy lover, a poor father, and a bad provider. She called him constantly and even e-mailed him vituperative messages. It reached the point at which he told his lawyer that he would give her anything she wanted just to get her off his back.

When verbal abuse is a relatively recent development, the best response from a legal perspective is to monitor it. If the verbal attacks continue without abating or intensifying, you should talk to your lawyer about whether they constitute abuse and can be stopped with a restraining order or an order of protection.

In most cases, though, your best strategy is to recognize that once the divorce goes through, the verbal attacks will probably diminish—although in some cases they may escalate into physical abuse. Be as calm as you can in the face of these attacks. Don't become embroiled in screaming matches. Besides making you feel worse, getting sucked into the hostility will only render you more vulnerable to your spouse's demands and increase the likelihood of physical altercations.

Be aware, too, that sometimes these attacks begin at the start of the divorce process and diminish as the process unfolds. People can be furious at the beginning and vent their anger verbally, but after a while, they may come to their senses and stop the abuse on their own.

2. Is there an explicit demand that is part of the abuse?

When your spouse is hurling every profanity in the book, is he also telling you that "I deserve the house" or "I should be able to see the kids whenever I want"? If so, the odds are that this abuse is calculated; it is designed to prey on your fears, doubts, and guilt to achieve a specific goal.

You can turn this type of abuse to your advantage by talking to your lawyer about the specific things your spouse wants. It may be that you can use this as a negotiating ploy, conceding a point in exchange for something you want.

Whatever you do, don't make this concession simply as a response to the negative feelings engendered by the abuse. As tempting as it may be to end the abuse by acquiescing to the demand, simply tell him, "I'll think about it."

3. How is the abuse affecting your children?

Are your children frightened by your spouse's angry words? Are they being made to feel guilty, as if they are responsible for causing the divorce? Do they return from a visit with your spouse sullen, in tears, angry, or upset in any way?

Your spouse may be taking out her anger at you on your kids, and this is unacceptable. Don't let her verbally torture your children in order to wrest concessions from you. Document what is taking place; tape-record phone calls and other conversations if lawful. Keep recordings of all threatening and abusive messages left on your voice mail. Courts may act to prevent verbal abuse of children, but only if this abuse is adequately documented and brought to their attention. This needs to be done in a strategic and timely fashion in conjunction with your lawyer.

4. Do you believe the verbal abuse is a sign of a more serious problem that will escalate even after the divorce is final?

Admittedly, this can be a tough call to make. Still, if you believe your spouse has a serious psychological problem—for example, if you believe she's bipolar, that she has anger management problems, or that her verbal abuse may turn physical—then you need to take action. You don't want your children to be alone with someone who is unstable and might harm them psychologically or physically.

A word of caution is in order here: Be aware that if you communicate with your spouse's psychiatrist (rather than your own), the doctor-patient privilege does not exist for you—you are not the doctor's patient. What goes on in joint sessions that include you, your spouse, and your doctor can be used in court against you as well, because a privilege waiver exists when your spouse is present. Therefore, be very careful what you say—you should probably talk to your attorney about dos and don'ts during these sessions. For instance, if you issue threats and vow to destroy your spouse's life during these joint sessions, these statements can come back to haunt you in court. At the same time, you may use your spouse's statements during these joint sessions to prove that she is neglectful, a drug user, or whatever else she will admit to.

5. Do you suspect that your spouse may be capable of physical abuse?

Many verbally abusive people are capable of becoming physically abusive, given the right circumstances and personality type. Even if your spouse has confined his abuse to words, you need to consider seriously whether it's likely that he will resort to physical violence. To facilitate this consideration, do the following:

- Have your lawyer conduct a background check of your spouse. Was your spouse married before and you didn't know it? Were there orders of protection or restraining orders against him? Has he ever been arrested for a violent act? Is there a history of drinking or drug abuse (which increases the odds of physical abuse) that you didn't know about?

- Document the verbal abuse for threats of physical action, such as, "You say that again and you're going to regret it," or, "If you don't let me have visitation every weekend, I'm going to kill you." Don't assume threats are empty; alert your lawyer to any threats made against you or your children.

- Monitor your children's physical condition when they return from visits with your spouse. If you have young children and the other parent has struck them in anger, they may not tell you about it—they may feel they deserved it or your spouse may have threatened them with consequences if they were to tell. After a visit, watch for any unusual bruises or cuts; signs children have been crying; or unusual behavior.

If you experience or witness physical abuse, or even if you only suspect it, one of the worst mistakes you can make is to alert an abuser of scrutiny. When abusers are told they may be reported, or if they are served with a petition for injunctive relief, these actions can trigger a violent episode, and you may end up hurt. Therefore, don't threaten to report the physical abuser, assuming that she can't do anything because the divorce will soon be completed. The court date may be in two weeks but then may be continued for another month, giving the abuser plenty of time to act on her violent urges.

This is another case where an emergency ex parte court action may work wonders to ensure that your spouse isn't jolted into action. As a general rule, avoid restraining orders or injunctions in abuse cases unless no other options exist, because if they are violated, the only remedies are civil. A restraining order can work well for protecting property, but we're talking about your physical safety here. You need an Emergency Ex Parte Order of Protection. These orders can be enforced criminally.

If you call the police and tell them your spouse is violating a restraining order, they'll often tell you to call your lawyer because it is a civil matter. But an order of protection provides a criminal solution; the police are likely to respond immediately, and intervene before the situation escalates. Be aware, though, that when you obtain the order of protection, it is only a piece of paper until you take further action. You need to inform the local police, and give a copy to your children's schools and daycare providers to ensure that they don't release the child to your spouse if such conduct is prohibited.

Here are a few other words of warning if you feel your spouse is physically abusive:

Make sure your lawyer is fully aware that your spouse has the capacity to be violent

It's your lawyer's responsibility to do everything possible to ensure your safety, but if he is not aware that your spouse may be physically abusive, he cannot help you. In one extreme case, a wife agreed to give her husband access to the marital home during the divorce process to pick up his personal possessions. The wife neglected to tell her lawyer about the agreement, as well as about her husband's rage. When the police escorted him to the house, they waited in the car. He went immediately to his dresser, got his gun, and shot and killed her. Then he left the house and told the police that he was done and they could take him away.

Both men and women can be guilty of physical abuse. This behavior is not gender-specific

I once hired a detective who set up a hidden video camera to document my client's claim of continued physical abuse by his wife, and we taped her attacking him viciously as soon as he returned home from work; the tape was very useful in criminal court to exonerate him of a bogus battery charge. In another case, an elderly man was being held captive in his own basement by his wife, who said she found it easier to take care of him that way. Women also have been known to abuse their children, and many kids have been harmed when it was assumed that mothers are not capable of this behavior.

Be aware that you or your children can be victimized by an abuser other than your spouse

Your spouse's boyfriend or girlfriend or even a relative can become so furious about the divorce that this unrelated adult becomes violent. I've even seen cases in which grandparents issued threats or became physically abusive.

THE AVENGER

Avengers are particularly difficult to deal with because they often act illogically; above all, they want to make your life hell, and they may even be willing to make their own lives hell in the process. These individuals are not concerned with what is best for your kids. They may not even be worried about getting the best settlement for themselves. Some may not even fear incarceration. Instead, they are driven only to avenge a perceived wrong. Lawyers often make mistakes when their clients' spouses are vengeful; they try to apply logic to negotiate a settlement, not recognizing that an avenger isn't likely to be logical. They are thus taken by surprise when the jerk rejects a fair settlement or takes off with the kids.

To assess whether your spouse is likely to be an avenger, consider whether any of the following apply to your situation:

❑ During your marriage, your spouse vowed vengeance if you ever divorced her.

❑ During your marriage, your spouse talked about how he had gotten revenge on someone (an employer, an ex-lover, or an enemy of some sort).

❑ Your spouse accused you of betrayal.

❑ You initiated the divorce proceedings because you met someone else, and told your spouse you never really loved her.

❑ Your spouse has threatened to make you or your kids suffer for what you're doing to him.

❑ In arguments during the marriage or the divorce process, your spouse has said, "You're going to pay for this" (or words to that effect).

If you can make check marks next to at least two of these items, then it is quite possible that your spouse will seek vengeance.

Vengeance can take many forms, but let's look at the three most common ways spouses seek it, and what you can do to protect yourself in each instance.

Visitation Vengeance

Custodial parents sometimes use visitation to torture their spouse, playing around with dates and making excuses about why "now is not a good time." They may do this both during the divorce process and after the divorce is final. They may even fabricate stories about drunkenness, drug abuse, and licentious behavior, and ask the court to prohibit visitation or allow it only under strict supervision.

Sometimes people are gulled into believing that their spouse would never do anything so cruel. That may be true, until something sets her off, such as a particular demand your lawyer makes as part of the divorce settlement, or the news that you're seeing someone else.

Visitation is a relatively new phenomenon that seems to contribute to such over-the-top behavior. Many visitation orders being executed today are written in the spirit of fairness, calling for unlimited visitation on a mutually agreeable and reasonable basis, to be determined in a cooperative manner that suits all the parties involved.

This is all well and good, as long as everybody feels like cooperating. But what happens if a change of circumstances occurs and your spouse suddenly feels vengeful? This is a situation in which you may be blindsided. The settlement seems fair, and everybody is reasonably happy. The couple has gotten past all the feuding and fighting and recriminations, and are even almost friends again. Friends, that is, until one of them becomes involved in a new relationship.

In many divorces, even though the legal machinery has functioned admirably and the divorce is completed in accordance with the court and the law of the land, the divorce—in the deepest sense—never has been completed. Yes, the papers have been signed, sealed, and delivered, but the emotional separation has never really taken root. Strangely enough, the post-divorce healing process may be working a bit too well—so well, in fact, that someone may be harboring fantasies about resuming the relationship or even the marriage. Then, when the other individual suddenly becomes involved with someone else, it's a shot across the bow. It can seem like adultery in spite of the divorce, and that's when vengeance may rear its ugly head. False child-abuse charges may be filed and visitation be temporarily suspended. Or at the very least, the vengeful spouse may invent excuses why you can't see your children.

If you suspect your spouse may be vengeful, do the following:

- **Make sure that the visitation order spells everything out.** It's difficult, time-consuming, and emotionally draining to get out the calendars and negotiate every single day along with all the holidays, birthdays, and special occasions. But if you don't, you're asking for trouble. Too many visitation agreements are vague, incomplete, or unenforceable, and contain flowery language providing a vengeance-seeking custodial parent with the opportunity to play games with visitation. For instance, reasonable visitation may not be enforceable because people differ as to the definition of "reasonable." Similarly, unlimited visitation as agreed to by the parties is not enforceable if the parties do not agree.

- **Anticipate that your spouse may use your children as a weapon against you and address safeguards during settlement negotiations.** Have a pro-child visitation conversation with your lawyer. Talk about how you view visitation as sacred and insist on language in the settlement agreement enjoining your spouse from using it manipulatively. If your spouse has demonstrated the capacity to create trouble in these situations, you must have case-specific prohibitions spelled out to protect you and your children. For example, if your spouse customarily attacks you in the children's presence, a prohibition would limit this behavior under penalty of forfeiting the visitation. If your spouse agrees to being enjoined against specific conduct, it may carry weight later on as part of a court order. Psychologically, this often can be an effective hedge against vengeful behavior.

Vengeance Through Kidnapping

A tactic to exact vengeance is fleeing with the children, a behavior that often accompanies severe emotional stress. Though uncommon, kidnapping seems to be increasing in frequency during acrimonious divorces. In one case, my client and his ex had a seemingly ideal post-divorce relationship. He paid for everything, as he had done during the marriage, and took pains to strengthen his bond with the children. Then he abruptly announced he was remarrying, and the bubble burst. In severe emotional turmoil, his ex-wife took the children to another state the night before the wedding. When the kids phoned him, they said, "We're fine, but Mom said we can't tell you where we are."

If he has family outside the United States and there is intense marital conflict, be aware that your spouse may kidnap the children during the divorce process and flee the country. If your spouse feels that the best way to punish you is by denying you contact with your kids, he may round them up and flee without thinking about the consequences. Certain events in the divorce process can trigger kidnapping as vengeance, such as:

- As part of the settlement, you say that you will allow your spouse to visit with the kids only on a limited basis under close supervision, or prohibit all visitation.

- In court, you testify in convincing fashion to your spouse's negative impact on the kids and why you want sole custody.

- Your spouse believes that the settlement or court decision will not punish you sufficiently.

You need evidence that your spouse might kidnap the kids if you want the court to act by enjoining such conduct, especially if your spouse is the custodial parent. Proof can consist of anything from secretly making reservations for three (if you have two kids) on a flight to another country during the divorce proceedings to a child relating a conversation in which one parent mentioned that "we're going to be moving away soon, but don't tell anyone." Many private investigators are skilled at confirming these suspicions and gathering proof.

If your spouse has relatives or contacts in another country and your children already have passports, you also may attempt to obtain a restraining order or order of protection with language specifically prohibiting your spouse from removing your children from the state and the country. Furthermore, you may seek a court order for your spouse to turn over the children's passports to the court immediately (that day) and further enjoin this parent from obtaining duplicate passports. With such an order, you then send correspondence to the U.S. Department of State, Office of Passport Policy and Advisory Services, Passport Services. Your cover letter must request that duplicate U.S. passports not be issued, and that you be notified immediately if reissuance of passports occurs in violation of the court order. Make sure you send the letter by certified mail so you have proof it was received. The State Department can list your children in a passport lookout database and alert you when an application for a passport is made in their names.

Vengeance Through the Legal Process

If your spouse is particularly wealthy or particularly perverse, she can use the legal process to exact her proverbial pound of flesh. This type of avenger relishes making you jump through legal hoops; she gets a weird kick out of forcing you to give lengthy depositions and making outrageous demands or filing outlandish charges. She will lie and tell the court you abused your children, enjoying your embarrassment. She may want nothing more than her day in court so she can tell the world what a scumbag you are.

Similarly, some people use the legal process to increase the financial pressure you feel. This is especially true when one parent works and the other doesn't. The working spouse may use his financial clout to increase your legal fees, drawing the legal process out to cost you money you can't afford. He may argue over every nickel and dime you jointly possess, demanding an heirloom that you care deeply about and that he has never even looked at.

If you're facing this type of avenger recognize the following truth:

The more you fight and scream, the more pleasure the jerk gets.

Therefore, don't fan the flames. Don't match accusation with accusation. Instead, give in on the little things. Focus on the big picture. Instruct your lawyer to do everything possible to avoid unnecessary court appearances (as they will ratchet up the expenses unnecessarily) and work diligently to reach a settlement. Recognize, too, that many people quickly tire of petty accusations and outrageous charges if you're not willing to play their game.

THE TEMPORARY-OR-PERMANENT QUESTION

We've saved this question for last because it's the most difficult one to answer. People say and do horrible things at the start of divorce proceedings but sometimes regret their words and deeds and become more reasonable as the process unfolds. Others are unrepentant and mean-spirited, and they remain jerks for years.

In some ways, whether your spouse's behavior is temporary or permanent doesn't matter. You still have to respond from a legal standpoint, and there's no way of knowing if he'll come to his senses. At the same time, if you suspect the behavior is temporary, you can use a number of tactics to give your spouse the opportunity to cease his bad behaviors, including:

- **Having your lawyer buy you some time through various legal maneuverings, such as asking for various delays or using mediation.** Generally, the longer the process drags on, the more opportunity your spouse has to vent his anger and come to his senses.

- **Going to counseling separately or together—especially if you have failed to seek help before the break up.** In any divorce, one spouse usually has years of pent-up anger, disappointment, sadness, and other emotions that he has never expressed—or has never expressed to his satisfaction. When divorce papers are filed, these emotions intensify and can create temporary jerk behavior. Therapy doesn't always work, but it may allow your spouse to let off some steam, which may help moderate his lousy behavior.

- **Being flexible and willing to compromise . . . to a point.** Obviously, you don't want to give away your property, kids, or anything else of importance. The more reasonable you are, however, the more likely a temporary jerk will see the light of day and stop torturing you. If your spouse is insisting that he rather than you take your son to his baseball games, give in on that point (unless you feel there is some danger to your child). If your spouse is hurting for money and you can afford it, lend or give him a little. These gestures will mean something to an essentially good person who temporarily is acting badly.

To determine the likelihood of these three tactics being effective, I've created a list of questions designed to separate temporary from permanent jerks. The more yes answers you have, the more likely that you're dealing with someone who is a jerk down to her toenails:

- Before you got married, did your friends warn you about your spouse and urge you not to marry her?

- Thinking back on your spouse's behaviors, did she always put herself before your needs or those of your children?

- Does your spouse have a history of doing mean things to others?

- In hindsight, do any behaviors you deemed kind or decent during your marriage now seem manipulative?

- Did your spouse control and punish you or your kids (for example, refusing to give you money for dinner because of something you said) for what she described as disrespectful or hurtful behavior?

- Do you feel that you were living with someone who was acting the part of a good spouse, but who was never really genuine when it came to her feelings for you or your children?

- Did your spouse verbally or physically abuse you or the children during the marriage?

- Once you informed your spouse you wanted a divorce, did it seem like she was acting "real" for the first time?

- Was your spouse unreasonable about money before you started divorce proceedings?

- Has your spouse's behavior during the divorce process confirmed what you've always suspected about her?

Knowing whether your spouse is a permanent or temporary jerk or if she is prone to money manipulation, abuse, or vengeance behaviors will give you an edge as you move through the divorce. You may even be able to use this knowledge to keep the divorce from turning into an all-out war. As you'll discover, it's possible to arrive at a settlement agreement with people who exhibit even the worst behaviors.

CHAPTER FIVE

How to Settle
a Difficult Divorce

The good news is that even contentious divorces can be and are settled, avoiding the cost and emotional trauma that accompany litigation. The bad news is that many tough cases that *can* be settled aren't, primarily because one or both parties don't take advantage of savvy settlement strategies.

My goal here is to share these strategies with you. Ideally, no matter how difficult people may be acting, these strategies will help them come to their senses. I have been involved in many cases where husbands and wives were at each other's throats and ignoring the best interests of their children, but through negotiation were able to reach agreements that satisfied everyone.

I don't want to make the negotiation process sound overly simple. It's not. When one person is furious at the other person's behavior—when he thinks she's ruined his life by having an affair or she thinks he's turned her children against her—it can be a steep climb toward settlement. I should add that there are circumstances in which cases cannot and should not be settled. You may have a spouse who is a danger to you or your children, who is demanding sole custody despite the fact that you are sure she'll be a negligent parent or drinks to the point that she can't function effectively as a parent. It may also be that your spouse is so angry at you that he refuses to pay one penny in child support or has managed to hide a great deal of his income.

In these instances, litigation may be a better approach than settlement. Still, given the costs and stress of going to trial, settlement options should be explored. The first step in this exploration is making it clear to your attorney what your goals are for the divorce and what you are and are not willing to accept.

WHAT YOU WANT VERSUS WHAT IS REALISTIC

No matter how good your attorney is, he is likely to deliver an unsatisfactory result unless he knows what your divorce goals are. General goals are insufficient. He must have a very specific idea of what you want in terms of property, custody arrangements, and so on; he must also grasp what you absolutely won't accept in these key areas. In this way, he can enter negotiation with a purpose and a plan. Without them, he is flying by the seat of his pants and can mistakenly agree to terms that won't meet your requirements.

To help you determine your goals, here are the key areas you must address and questions related to each that will help you assess what is and is not acceptable:

Custody

- Is joint custody the only acceptable option?

- Will you accept only sole custody because you feel your spouse is a danger to your child?

- Will you allow your spouse to have custody if you are given a favorable visitation schedule and other parental rights?

- Do you have specific custody-related requirements regarding where your child lives, vacations, parental authority on key decisions involving your child, and restrictions on where your spouse can move (if she is the custodial parent)?

Child Support

- Are you willing and able to pay the state-mandated norm?

- Are there reasons you feel that your spouse should pay or exceed the norm?

- Do you have any concerns or needs regarding your share of your child's college tuition?

- Are there any issues regarding private school tuition or your share of any big-ticket items for your child (such as a musical instrument or private lessons of any type)?

Visitation

- What do you feel is a fair visitation schedule for you or your spouse?

- Do you want more visitation than the norm? Do you want your spouse to have less? Why?

- Are you going to insist on supervised visitation for your spouse?

Community Property

- If you and your spouse own property (such as a house, condo, summer home, or land), what do you feel is a fair division of this asset?

- How much flexibility do you have regarding the division of property? For example, would you be willing to let your spouse have the house in exchange for more favorable visitation terms?

- Is there a particular piece of property that you feel you are entitled to and that you absolutely refuse to give to your spouse or sell?

- Are there other assets that you feel you are entitled to and that your spouse should not have (such as a valuable painting given to you by a close friend)?

- Are there tangible assets that you know your spouse wants and that you would be willing to use as "barter" to achieve other divorce goals?

Financial Assets

- Do you and your spouse have pension, profit-sharing, or other benefits plans? What do you believe would be a fair division of these plan assets?

- Do you and your spouse own stocks and bonds, or have other investments? What do you believe is a fair division of these assets?

- How much money do you have in various accounts, and how do you believe this money should be divided?

- Are you willing to give your spouse more of a share of these financial assets than the law dictates in exchange for something else (or do you want more in exchange for giving your spouse other things)?

This is just a partial list of questions and categories, but it will help you start thinking about some important issues. To a certain extent, you're at the mercy of the laws of your state. If you're the sole wage earner and you've been married for a number of years and have a few kids, you will be asked to provide a specific amount of child support and possibly maintenance. At the same time, many of these issues are negotiable. What you must do is figure out what works for you. I ask my clients to provide me with a wish list. In other words, I suggest that they not worry about what's possible and just tell me what they want from the divorce. With that list in mind, we then talk about what's possible, given legal realities and the particular difficulties a spouse is likely to pose. If the wish list is ridiculous—say, if someone wants all the assets and sole custody just because his spouse wants the divorce— I explain that this isn't going to happen. We then try to arrive at a modified wish list, taking all factors into consideration.

To help you consider these factors and modify your wish list, the first step is to assess how your spouse is likely to make the divorce difficult. In Chapter 4, we identified three basic categories of difficulty: money, abusiveness, and vengeance. Knowing whether your spouse is going to cause problems in one of these areas can be valuable in determining your legal strategy. If, for instance, you know your spouse is a penny-pincher and is going to fight tooth and nail over everything of monetary value and may even resort to hiding assets, you may be able to prevent some of these behaviors, or at least moderate them. It may be worth it to you to give up your rights to the fancy sports car and the summer home in order to avoid costly litigation and an emotionally draining divorce process.

The next step is to figure out where you stand on these issues versus your spouse. Whether or not your spouse has also created a wish list, he likely has one in the back of his mind. There are issues that he won't budge on and assets to which he feels he's entitled. You will greatly strengthen your legal case if you and your lawyer evaluate how strong your legal position is as well as how strong your spouse's position is. Even the most difficult spouse is usually amenable to negotiation if you're negotiating from a position of strength. If, on the other hand, your spouse is in the power position, you may have to modify your negotiation tactics accordingly. You can't realistically expect to litigate sole custody successfully if your husband has been a good parent, has never abused or endangered your child in any way, and has been a stay-at-home dad, and you have not visited your child since she was born. In this area, at least, your spouse is in a position of strength.

To help your attorney evaluate your strengths and weaknesses, answer the following questions:

- **Would you term your position strong, average, or weak relative to what you want to achieve?** In other words, do you have evidence that supports your desire for sole custody or that provides compelling proof that you should receive child support above the norm? Do you have credible experts, such as accountants, doctors, and therapists, who will testify on your behalf regarding all relevant issues?

- **Is your spouse in a vulnerable position when it comes to negotiation issues?** For instance, does she have a criminal record? Has she ever been arrested for physical abuse of the children? Does she have a drug problem for which she's been in treatment, or an emotional or psychological disorder for which she's taken medication? Has she violated a restraining order and abused you or tried to abscond with the children?

- **Is there something your spouse wants above all else from the divorce that you would be willing to provide in exchange for other concessions?** Does she most want to avoid returning to the workforce? Does she want to make sure you never move and take her children out of the area in which she lives, making it more difficult for her to see them? Is your home her dream house, and does she want it more than any other asset?

- **Do you know or suspect that your spouse intends to make changes in her life that will potentially affect negotiations?** Do you suspect that she intends to remarry shortly after the divorce? If so, will her new husband have significant financial assets? Does your spouse intend to move to another state after the divorce for work or other reasons? Does she hope to retire soon?

- **Do you believe your spouse will be rational about the various issues that come up during negotiations?** If not, are there certain hot-button issues that you need to avoid or downplay? Is she so vengeful that she won't listen to reason or participate in negotiations? Is she so abusive (physically or emotionally) that she can't be in the same room as you during the negotiation process? Is she so penurious or greedy that money will be the sticking point in negotiations?

I realize that you may have answered some of these questions earlier, but I wanted to emphasize them and be sure that they weren't skipped. With these answers articulated to your attorney, you're now ready to negotiate for what you want.

HOW TO NEGOTIATE PAST OBSTACLES

Negotiation can take two forms: formal and informal. The latter often involves ad hoc conversations between attorneys in courtroom hallways, sometimes as early as right after divorce papers are filed. Assuming you have children and assets in common, you probably are going to be talking to your spouse during the process; you may each emphasize what you want, and one of you may suggest a compromise. Sometimes, negotiation stalemates are better resolved informally than formally. People can become anxious and hold tight to their positions when attorneys are present and the process is intimidating. They might loosen up when they are at home making a phone call to their spouse. Therefore, don't rule out informal negotiation as an option.

Realistically, however, some divorces begin with accusations and threats, discouraging informal negotiations. It may be in your best interest to start off with a formal negotiation session, which your attorney and your spouse's attorney can set up. Expect the start of the session to be frustrating. Difficult divorces usually mean that one party starts out asking for almost everything and the other starts out willing to give up almost nothing. If your spouse is abusive, he may begin with a list of your sins as justification for his demands. If he is vengeful, he may threaten you with the loss of your kids. If he is money-crazed, he may propose a deal in which he gets everything and you get nothing.

If you want the negotiation process to move forward rather than go directly into a litigation phase, you must do the following:

- **Take the other side's opening offer with a grain of salt.**
  Don't overreact to an outrageously unreasonable offer. In fact, expect it. It may be that your spouse is crazed and won't back off, but it's also possible that this is simply a legal gambit. Respond with a counteroffer and without an emotional outburst and see where the negotiation goes from there.

- **Know where you're willing to compromise, and do so when the time is right.** If you're dug in as deep as your spouse, you're never never going to settle anything. Therefore, use the previous exercises so both you and your attorney have cards to play. Decide that you're willing to trade A for B. This gives your attorney room to negotiate. It may be that your offer of helping your spouse defray his expenses to get his graduate degree will break a deadlock about how often you get to see your kids.

- **Step out of the room when your presence is doing more harm than good.** I had a client who threw a glass of water in his spouse's face; the dispute escalated and the police were called. Clearly, my client was unable to keep his cool, and the negotiation process would have been better served if he (and his spouse) were not at the table. I realize that it's difficult to step away from the negotiating table, but sometimes it's necessary in difficult divorces. The wounds are too fresh, the tension is too high, and one or both people are too angry, vengeful, or irrational. A couple's roiling emotions often sabotage the best efforts to negotiate in good faith.

Ideally, these techniques will move you toward a settlement. What happens, however, if you're willing to compromise but your spouse is not? What can you do if your husband or wife is being incredibly difficult? Here are some approaches that I've found to be effective under certain circumstances.

First, your lawyer can engage in "creative discovery." For instance, I represented a woman whose husband had a cash business and claimed he had no business records, and it was easy for him to disguise the business's true value as well as his income. During negotiations, he told my client that his business was worthless, so he couldn't pay child support or give her any money for maintenance. I tried to break the stalemate through discovery.

I subpoenaed for a deposition just about everyone he did business with (including his customers) and obtained this information from his private cell phone records through discovery. My client was absolutely certain that her husband's business was worth a considerable amount of money, and this creative discovery was like firing a warning shot. My client's husband was furious that we were subpoenaing his customers; he also must have suspected that we would uncover all sorts of information about his business practices and income. Whether we would have been able to pinpoint the exact value of his business turned out be a moot point. He wanted us to cease and desist our inquiries, and he offered fair child support, maintenance payments, and a property settlement to my client if we promised to end our investigations immediately.

Second, encourage your lawyer to "counterpunch" when appropriate rather than going on the defensive. If your spouse is truly difficult—if he's vindictive and crazed—he's capable of all sorts of legal stunts. *He may attempt to have you declared an unfit mother, or he may ask the court for a baseless order of protection.* For the sake of the negotiation, a lawyer may advise his client that the best thing to do is file a response quietly and avoid doing anything to further inflame the situation. This is good advice in certain situations. Sometimes, however, it is the worst possible thing to do. Some difficult people relish putting their spouse on the defensive. As long as they can torture their husband or wife in this manner and have nothing to lose, they are happy. They believe this offensive strategy gives them the upper hand during negotiations. I've found that in these instances, counterpunching helps the wronged party regain her footing. If someone files a false pleading seeking an unfair advantage against you, perhaps you should file a fee petition and seek sanctions against him for filing a false pleading. For the negotiation to proceed, you may need to achieve something that is the equivalent of nuclear détente—you want the other side to know you possess powerful weapons and you don't want to use them, but you will if pushed.

Third, if your spouse is taking actions that he should be embarrassed about, make sure he's aware that you're capable of embarrassing him. Your spouse may be horrified at the thought of his many affairs or his unwillingness to support your kids being made public. During negotiations, though, he may operate under the assumption that you'd never allow the details of your marital problems to become common knowledge. He may believe that you'll settle because you don't want to go through the spectacle of a public trial. Disabuse him of that notion. Make sure he knows that you're fully capable of communicating to his parents, siblings, and friends the truth about his behavior. If he's acting like a jerk during negotiations, this realization may cause him to be less jerklike and more accommodating.

A number of years ago, I represented the wife of a professional athlete who was making huge sums of money. During the initial negotiations, I suggested that the wife wanted a trust started for his young children for their future college expenses and an appropriate level of child support. His attorney said to forget about the trust and that this multimillionaire athlete would pay only $2,000 in monthly child support, which was far below the minimum child support guidelines. It was clear that the husband was dug into this position, even though it was ridiculous. Maybe he wanted to punish his wife for real or imagined wrongs, or maybe he was just cheap. Whatever the reason, no amount of reasoning could make him up the offer. At that time, however, I had a show on the local ESPN radio station, and I mentioned during one of the negotiation conferences that wealthy athletes who father and fail to support their children adequately would make an interesting topic for the show. I suspect the fear of public exposure and embarrassment and the potential loss of millions of dollars in product endorsements did the trick. The husband became much more reasonable, and the case settled quickly.

WHY CASES DON'T ALWAYS
SETTLE WHEN THEY SHOULD

Divorce cases blow up all the time during negotiations. Sometimes, there's nothing you can do about these blowups except go to trial. In other instances, however, these cases could have been settled if one of the parties had taken or avoided some simple actions. Let's look at four common causes of blowups involving potentially explosive divorces and what you can do if you're facing similar situations:

1. **Bad timing.** During the divorce process, there are moments when one or both people are extremely vulnerable or under great stress. It may be that a work problem is causing one spouse a lot of grief, or one of them is dealing with a medical issue or wrestling with a tough financial decision. Whatever the issue, you should not exploit this moment by filing an unnecessary motion against your spouse or making an unreasonable demand when the case is ready to settle on reasonable terms. I once represented a surgeon who was in the process of getting divorced, and the case was rapidly moving toward a settlement. His wife, however, filed a motion with the court asking for increased financial support while the divorce was in process, and he was served with it only minutes before he had one of the

most important surgeries of his professional life scheduled. He was furious and insisted on going to trial on every issue. Similarly, pay attention to what you say and do around your spouse during a stressful period. It's not just legal actions that can destroy the delicate negotiations. Your spouse is especially likely to overreact if you push his buttons while he's under pressure. For instance, if you have a vengeful spouse who is going through a tough period, you don't want to show up at your child's school's open house with your new boyfriend on your arm. This may seem like common sense, but people often don't realize how fragile some negotiations are and do something that they feel is innocuous but strikes their spouse as done deliberately to provoke.

2. **Giving up on negotiation.** People sometimes forsake trying to settle their case because of a fight about who gets what. Negotiations become tense, one spouse becomes upset, and the parties move toward a trial. Be aware, however, that a settlement is possible up until that moment the judge makes a decision. People often don't realize that even after a trial starts, it is perfectly acceptable to reach a settlement. Obviously, it's more difficult to settle in the middle of a trial, but both spouses may come to their senses once the trial begins and be more flexible about overcoming the issues that previously prevented a settlement.

3. **Refusing to see a therapist.** It is amazing to me when negotiations break down between two people who aren't very far apart on the major issues. The cause of the breakdown is emotional. One person may have a deep and abiding hatred for the other person, and this hatred may prevent them from

agreeing on even the simplest of issues. In some instances, a couple needs to bite the bullet and bring in a therapist before continuing with negotiations. I've found that if one person is mired in depression, is seething with hostility, or has some other psychological issue, it is difficult for that person to get past the issue and negotiate like a rational human being. Therapy must be used responsibly rather than manipulatively. While it has its limits, it also is capable of calming people down sufficiently so they can return to the bargaining table with a renewed sense of purpose.

4. **Ignoring the judge.** Contrary to many people's expectations, judges want cases to settle, preferably before the trial begins. In fact, judges usually will be inclined to share with attorneys what they expect to decide if the case goes to trial based on the anticipated evidence. This preliminary opinion can jar one or both parties into settlement mode. In some cases, both attorneys will be frustrated because they know they have a case that can be settled, but their clients are being unreasonable. In these instances, they can ask the judge to speak to their clients before the trial begins and exert his authority in order to help them reach a settlement. Therefore, pay attention to what judges say and be open to meeting with them prior to the trial.

THE ROAD TO REASON: MEDIATION

Some divorces can't be mediated. Warring partners may be so crazed about money, so bent on vengeance, or so abusive that mediation is like trying to stop a flood with a few sandbags. Mediation works best when both people are relatively reasonable and able (with the assistance of the mediator) to see past their conflict and do what is best for their kids. Nonetheless, I've also seen mediation work during divorce wars. Sometimes it works because of the mediator's skill. Other times it functions effectively because the process itself helps take some of the edge off hurtful emotions.

Let's start out by defining mediation. Mediation involves a facilitator, or mediator, who assists both parties in reaching a settlement. Typically, its main goal is to resolve custody disputes. In fact, a significant number of states require or recommend mediation to deal with these disputes. Mediation, though, can address any matter of contention in a divorce. Mediators may be lawyers or judges, but they don't have to be. Therapists often are mediators, and it's not unusual to find a clergyman serving this role. While mediation can last for weeks or months, anywhere from two to five sessions are the norm. During these sessions, a mediator attempts to guide a couple through the tough issues they're struggling with and help them reach an agreement on them. He may bring in the couple's children as part of the process. He may even invite their lawyers to attend (though more commonly, people consult with lawyers before and after the sessions). I should emphasize that mediation is not an adversarial process. The mediator should be impartial, and he should help a couple reach a settlement that the lawyers then put into a legal document after the mediation is completed and present to the court for final approval. Once the judge signs the document, it becomes a binding court order.

The mediation process can vary from mediator to mediator, but it typically proceeds in the following way:

1. **Setting ground rules.** Essentially, the mediator educates the couple about what the process will involve, emphasizing

the importance of setting aside feelings in favor of best-interest-of-the-child compromises, being flexible, and respecting the other person.

2. **Placing the real issues on the table.** Each person clearly states what he or she is willing to accept in terms of a settlement. Much of what a mediator does is identify the real obstacles to an agreement, obstacles that are often obscured by anger and posturing. The mediator attempts to state each person's position clearly and without emotional baggage.

3. **Articulating problem-solving options.** Many times, negotiations outside of mediation become bogged down because people are stuck in their positions. The mediator suggests alternatives that both parties may never have considered. She articulates concerns about these alternatives and facilitates discussions that allow both people to understand what each alternative entails.

4. **Refining and solidifying solutions.** Once both spouses agree in principle on a solution, the mediator restates and refines this solution, making sure they both accept its more specific articulation. She helps them create a written document that can be used by their lawyers to forge a legally binding settlement. While the results of mediation aren't legally binding, the solutions it forges can help lawyers resolve even the most difficult of divorce situations.

Be aware that mediators usually tell people that whatever they say in mediation is confidential, but in reality this isn't always the case, especially if the mediator is a therapist. Therapists are mandated reporters, which means they are required by law to report suspected child abuse, even if they're not certain abuse exists. Therefore, recognize that you may say something during a session that the mediator misinterprets and ends up reporting as abuse. If the mediator is skilled and perceptive, this shouldn't happen, but mediators, like lawyers, come with varying levels of competency.

In divorce wars, mediation generally works better in certain situations than in others. Read the following list and place a check mark if a situation applies to you:

- ❏ A great deal of finger-pointing and name-calling are preventing the negotiation process from moving forward.
- ❏ One or both parties are locked into unreasonable positions and absolutely refuse to compromise.
- ❏ Both parents genuinely want to do what is best for their kids but have different definitions of what is best.
- ❏ One or both parties refuse to acknowledge alternatives for settlement beyond the one they are stuck on.
- ❏ Attorneys are exacerbating the bad feelings between parents because they are overly antagonistic and argumentative.
- ❏ Poor communication is causing misinterpretation of each party's position, causing blowups.
- ❏ You have reached agreement in principle on many issues, but one or two issues are stalling negotiations.

If you've made at least one check mark, mediation may help resolve the difficulties you face. On the other hand, mediation may be ineffective if you check one or more items on the following list:

- ❏ On a scale of 1 to 10 (with 10 being the most intense), your spouse is at the high end when it comes to being abusive, vengeful, or money-crazy.

❑ Your spouse's number-one goal for the divorce is to punish you.

❑ Your spouse is a danger to you or your children; given the opportunity, he will hurt you or them, or kidnap them.

❑ You know your spouse is hiding assets and will lie and commit fraud in order to pay you and your children as little as possible.

❑ Your mediator is not particularly good at his job and makes a bad situation worse by being prejudiced in favor of one party.

❑ You are not particularly good at articulating your position (while your spouse is very articulate), resulting in mediation that favors your spouse rather than achieving a fair compromise.

❑ You or your spouse is not ready for mediation; you need more time to deal with the issues and perhaps therapy to get past the psychological obstacles to being able to talk about the issues objectively and with the best interests of the children in mind.

WHEN LAWYERS WOULD RATHER FIGHT THAN SETTLE

Be aware that it's not just vengeful spouses who blow up the negotiation process but also overly aggressive, self-interested attorneys. My intention is not to make you paranoid about lawyers, but to caution you about the small but significant percentage who make bad situations worse. Some of these lawyers are simply the victims of their nature and their profession: They became lawyers because they love to get in a good verbal fight, and they learned that being an aggressive, tough attorney can pay dividends. As a result, they push the other side too hard during negotiations and advise their clients not to settle, believing that they can get more for them if they draw a line in the sand or even if they have to go to trial. Other attorneys act this way because they want to churn their fees. They recognize that the more people they depose and the longer the trial lasts, the more money they'll make. And there are attorneys who rationalize going to trial as being best for their clients and their clients' kids, though if they were honest with themselves, they would see that they are making the process more complex and antagonistic for their own personal gain.

Clearly, you should avoid these types of attorneys, but that's not always possible. If you're furious at your spouse when you're searching for an attorney, you may be attracted to the one who promises to eviscerate her. You may also hire an attorney who talks about being reasonable and trying to negotiate a settlement but ends up pursuing a greedy, combative strategy.

Recognize that if you have a large marital estate or if you give your lawyer a substantial retainer fee, you may unwittingly be giving him an incentive to antagonize your spouse and her lawyer or to sandbag negotiations in order to go to trial. I've known more than one lawyer who received a $50,000 retainer fee after which negotiations raised the possibility of an early settlement. Recognizing that there was no way they could earn that fee if the divorce case settled quickly, they found a way to sabotage the negotiations, not only creating the need for a trial but increasing the tension between the couple and producing additional emotional trauma.

A few years ago, another attorney asked me to help him on a case in which he represented a woman with a $14 million marital estate. Her husband's attorney offered to settle the case by offering her 50 percent of the estate. This was a very fair offer, and I advised the woman to settle. My co-counsel, however, was furious with me. He urged his client to ignore my advice and convinced her that she was entitled to more and could get it if they went to trial. He also insisted that she dismiss me from the case because I'd advised her to settle, and she did. Ultimately, the case went to trial, and she was awarded 25 percent of the estate rather than the 50 percent originally offered, costing her millions of dollars. Her attorney, however, received a much higher fee than if the original offer had been accepted; no doubt he was well aware that this would be the outcome if he convinced her to go to trial.

Therefore, hold your attorney accountable for doing everything possible to settle the case. Pay attention to see if he is negotiating in good faith with opposing counsel. Observe whether their exchanges are collegial and professional or designed to antagonize. If negotiations break down, ask your attorney why: Is it because you've reached a true impasse and neither side will give an inch, or is it because he has provoked the other attorney or his client to the point that bargaining is no longer possible? If your attorney recommends that you go to trial, ask him why this is necessary. Question him about whether mediation might be a better interim step.

In addition, pay attention to the behaviors of both your attorney and opposing counsel. For instance, here's a ploy some attorneys use to create friction between opposing attorneys and their clients. Imagine you (as a divorcing spouse) just left the initial hearing, and you, your spouse, and both attorneys walk out together. Then your spouse's attorney says in a low, secretive voice to your attorney, "I'd like to talk to you in private." She leaves her client and walks with your attorney, and then they stop and talk with your spouse. Standing alone and observing the other three people talking, you think to yourself, "They're excluding me. They're conspiring against me." This paranoia may well translate into a more adversarial divorce process.

Unethical attorneys have other tricks to inflame simmering emotions in clients. For instance, an attorney is forbidden from speaking directly with the other attorney's client unless he receives permission to do so from that attorney. Yet it's not unusual for a lawyer to pass his client's spouse in a hallway or during a meeting and whisper loud enough for her to hear, "She's going to lose custody" or "The judge is going to put him in jail." Because the attorney said these things to his client, he hasn't technically committed an ethical breach, yet these whispered comments achieve his goal: His client's spouse becomes angry, upset, and anxious, increasing the tension between the couple and decreasing the chances of settlement.

Many people involved in difficult divorces are convinced that they are reasonable and want to settle but their spouses are stubborn jerks who want to go to court. In reality, both of you may want to settle, but your spouse's attorney may be turning down your request for a settlement conference. If you suspect that your spouse really does want to settle, then your attorney can use the following technique to try and make a settlement conference happen. Suggest that your attorney serve your spouse with a Notice of Deposition and have the deposition take place in your attorney's office. Your attorney can depose your spouse for the first hour or so (in some states, you are only allowed a maximum of three hours for a deposition unless you obtain court permission for an extension), but then may say something along the following lines: "If you want, we can continue this deposition at another time. But considering your client's testimony, it seems that if all of us just sat down and talked right now, we might be able to reach a settlement." While your spouse's attorney may remain resistant to this idea, your spouse may seize the opportunity even if his lawyer wants a war.

DOING EVERYTHING POSSIBLE
TO KEEP THE NEGOTIATIONS ALIVE

Sometimes there's nothing you can do. If your spouse is being impossible and acting irrationally, you may have no alternative but to go to trial and let a judge decide what should be done. Before you reach this point, however, you can try the following approaches to help your spouse come to her senses and remain at the bargaining table:

- **Reframe "me" arguments in "best-interest-of-the-child" terms.** Both you and your spouse may believe you're putting your children first, but your negotiation talks may inadvertently become all about the two of you—how each of you suffered, what one person did wrong, and so on. You may think or say, "I deserve joint custody because throughout our children's lives, I made career sacrifices to carry my fair share of the parenting responsibility." Recognize that from a custody negotiation standpoint, it's not about you. And making it about you only angers your spouse. Therefore, rephrase your argument as follows: "Our kids are used to my being there half the time and taking responsibility for everything from driving them to school to taking them to the doctor. It will help them get through the divorce and not be hurt by it if I can continue to do these things."

- **If you're the custodial parent, communicate to your spouse that his child-related goals for the divorce are connected to yours.** In other words, tell him that you will bend over backwards to make sure he sees his child frequently (assuming he has been a decent parent and his constant presence in the child's life is in the child's best interest). Explain that you need reasonable support or maintenance for you and the child. When this discussion becomes all about what one spouse wants for himself and what the other is willing to give, negotiations can stall. When the connection of mutual goals is made, settlement becomes a win-win process.

- **If you're the noncustodial parent, make the connection in the opposite direction.** In other words, explain how you provide strong financial support and expect to receive fair visitation arrangements and be involved in decisions regarding your kids.

- **Calculate projected costs if the case doesn't settle.** Even the most obstreperous people are sometimes motivated to return to the bargaining table when they review projected legal costs. When they see it in writing—when they realize how much they will have to pay for expert witnesses, various depositions, and all the hours racked up by their lawyers in a courtroom—they may have second thoughts about refusing to settle.

If these efforts don't work, then it's on to a trial. Trials involving spouses who are extremely vengeful, abusive, or money-crazed can be a nightmare, but there are ways to handle these situations to increase the odds that the results of the trial will be positive and its accompanying stress manageable.

CHAPTER SIX

Going to Court:
How to Make It Less of a Trial
and More of a Process

If negotiations have stalled or failed and you or your spouse
(or both of you) believe that the only way to resolve your differences is through a trial, be prepared to endure some financial and emotional blows. Unless you are tremendously wealthy
or amazingly stoic, you're probably going to encounter a certain
amount of unpleasantness as you get ready for your day in court.
It may become even more unpleasant when that day arrives.

Be aware, though, that you don't have to go through hell just
because you're going to court. You can limit the financial and emotional damage in a divorce war, and you can also take certain steps
to increase the odds that the judge's decision will be favorable.

I can't make the process painless for my clients, but I can advise
them how to avoid the trial-related pitfalls that so many divorcing

couples fall into, especially when vengeance, financial mania, or verbal or physical abuse factors into the mix. When people start seeing a trial as their moment of vindication or their chance to exact their pound of flesh, they're asking for trouble. When they go into divorce court unprepared or out of control, they will find themselves on the losing end of a judgment. And when they expect a favorable judgment because they're *obviously* in the right and their spouse is *obviously* in the wrong, they are mistakenly thinking that judges render decisions based on what's "obvious." It may be that your spouse is a cruel or unhinged individual; it may be that "everyone knows" he or she has done terrible things to you. This doesn't mean you'll get custody, or that you can prevent your spouse from seeing your kids, or that you'll receive exactly what you want from the marital or community property.

Let's start out, therefore, examining what you need to do to prepare for what's shaping up as a nasty trial, starting with depositions.

THE ART OF AN EFFECTIVE DEPOSITION

During the discovery phase before the trial, you and your attorney can gather all sorts of useful information or evidence that can be used during the trial. I've talked about how written interrogatories can be used to obtain information from your spouse and how they often are not of great value because your spouse had his lawyer help him answer the questions. You can also avail yourself of "requests for production" of documents involving everything from medical and financial records to your spouse's diary. In certain cases, evidence can be obtained that has a dramatic impact on the outcome of a trial. For instance, if you're in a bitter battle over custody, visitation, or money (how much one parent pays in child support, whether one spouse should return to work, who receives how much of the marital estate, and so on), the following pieces of evidence are key:

- A criminal conviction record involving drug use, domestic battery, or child abuse.

- Financial records that indicate your spouse has more money/assets than he admits to.

- A letter or legal document that indicates something your spouse says is her inheritance actually is marital or community property.

Earlier I noted that some spouses are permanent jerks while others only are temporary jerks, the latter being a passing condition caused by a divorce-related issue. Those in the first category are very difficult to deal with—they've always been insanely jealous, or the theme throughout their lives is vengeance. In these instances, you may be able to use the discovery process to prove that their bad behavior during your marriage is part of a pattern— a pattern that will have a bearing on a judge's decision. For instance, I had a client whose spouse was charging him with abusing their children as part of the divorce proceedings. She not only wanted sole custody but sought to prevent him from ever seeing their kids again. He denied these charges when we discussed this issue, and I believed his denial. Everything from his personality to his history to his relationship with his children suggested he was incapable of child abuse. He had a good job, came from a strong, supportive family, had never been arrested or charged with any crime, and clearly loved his kids, and they responded in kind. In short, he didn't fit the pattern of an abuser.

We decided to conduct a thorough search of his spouse's background to find evidence that she had made up these charges. We were looking for anything that might suggest she possessed this capacity—a record of drug or alcohol abuse, or a psychological problem or condition. Though our client was not aware of such records, he had known his wife for only five years, and she was now 40. He did know that she had a child from her first marriage, that her former husband was awarded custody, and that visitation was supervised. Though the search added to his legal costs, it was a gamble worth taking. We obtained the court file of her first divorce from a different county and found she had filed false child abuse charges against her former spouse in order to try to gain sole custody. Not only were those charges dismissed, but the court record showed that the wording of her abuse charges against her first spouse was remarkably similar to that of the charges filed against my client. As a result, the charges were eventually dropped and my client won custody.

While searching past records and requesting information can yield nuggets such as these, in difficult divorces oral depositions are often the most useful aspect of the discovery process. While depositions of all sorts of individuals can be useful, the deposition of a spouse is often critical. In a number of instances, I have seen cases turn on a spouse's oral deposition. What your spouse says *and does* when he is deposed in a lawyer's office can make a huge difference to a judge. I emphasize the word *does* because your spouse's demeanor in a videotaped deposition can make a difference if this videotape is played in court. If your spouse acts oddly or reacts violently to questions, this can have a bearing on a judge's decision.

Your spouse may also say something in a deposition that your lawyer can show to be false in court. For example, he may say that he doesn't have an anger management problem and has never been verbally or physically abusive toward you, your kids, or anyone else. In court, however, your lawyer may have a witness testify that she saw your spouse routinely berate you and your children using the most vile language possible and introduce records into evidence establishing that he was convicted of battery two years ago.

Deposing vengeful, money-crazed, and abusive spouses isn't easy. In many cases, they've been coached by their lawyer on what to say and how to act. Your spouse's lawyer is present when your lawyer takes his deposition. Nonetheless, certain techniques tend to produce good results. Here are three tactics I would recommend to anyone involved in a divorce war:

Have your attorney videotape the deposition

Some lawyers neglect to use video during depositions, feeling it's a lot of effort for little gain. This may be true in "normal" divorces, but in nasty ones, it can prove to be useful. Lawyers typically do a good job of preparing their clients for testifying in court, but they don't always do a good job of preparing them for their depositions. As a result, many people say and do things during depositions that can come back to haunt them. If your spouse is behaving like a lunatic or is so angry, vengeful, or money crazy that she can't control herself, then she may well lose her composure during a deposition. She won't necessarily lose the case because of this behavior, but it can have a profound effect on how the judge views your spouse and her claims. Your spouse's attorney may paint a picture of her as a model mom, but during the deposition she may be swearing like a sailor, throwing things at you, and making violent threats.

Recognize that your attorney usually can't play the entire video deposition in court to show the judge what your spouse is really like, unless it is an evidence deposition. Rules of evidence must be adhered to, but if your lawyer can catch your spouse in a contradiction when she's testifying in court, then you may have a sufficient basis to show the video to impeach her with the prior inconsistent statement. For instance, she may testify in court that she would never want to prevent you from seeing your children, while in the deposition, she threatened to make sure you never saw your children again unless you gave her the house, the car, and the boat.

Show your attorney how to push your spouse's buttons

Better than anyone else, you know your spouse's worst qualities and how they emerge during the divorce process. Is she obsessed with pushing you into bankruptcy through a long, drawn-out divorce process? Is she abusive and violent, and a danger to you and your children? Is she so focused on holding on to your dream house or avoiding rejoining the workforce that she'll make up any accusation to get what she wants? Is she only interested in separating you from your children, whether physically or emotionally?

Sharing these facts with your attorney will enable him to do a better job of getting your spouse to say something during the deposition that will hurt her case. If he's a sharp lawyer, he can use this information to push and prod your spouse, forcing her to lose her focus or give voice to her obsession. When people are in court, they have been thoroughly coached beforehand by their lawyers, and the controlled environment of the courtroom mitigates against their acting in self-destructive ways. During depositions, on the other hand, people want to blame, vent, and make demands. Given a little push, they may reveal why they are so difficult, and this can help you reveal the truth and receive a just settlement.

Get your attorney to start out trying to elicit a positive statement

One of the biggest mistakes attorneys making during depositions is being aggressive right from the start. An attorney who uses this tactic may antagonize and anger your spouse, making it unlikely that she'll say anything positive about you. I've found that in most cases, people retain some positive feelings for and memories about their spouse. Even in nasty divorces, people shared at least some good times and married their spouses because they admired certain traits they possessed. While the acrimony of divorce may obscure these traits, a skilled lawyer should be able to bring out at least some positive comments—that you were a good parent and a good provider, that you had great times on vacations with the kids, or that you sacrificed in some way for the good of the family.

Therefore, attorneys should be friendly and accommodating at the beginning of the deposition. If they need to push your spouse's buttons, they should do so later. You should tell your attorney what your positive qualities are—or at least what you think your spouse believes them to be. Think of specific things you've done or said during your marriage that your spouse appreciated, and share these specific incidents with your lawyer. He can then turn them into questions that might elicit positive remarks.

These positive statements can go a long way toward convincing a judge you're not the monster your spouse's attorney portrays and decrease the odds that he'll render a judgment befitting a monster.

Have your attorney make sure your spouse gets everything off her chest during the deposition and doesn't save anything for the trial

In other words, you want your spouse to state now rather than later all the reasons you shouldn't receive custody. You don't want her holding one key charge in reserve that she'll spring during the trial. In this way, your lawyer can be better prepared to counteract whatever charges are made against you. I recognize that this testimony can be unpleasant to listen to and may confuse clients. If you believe your spouse is a drinker and drug user and don't believe she should receive joint custody, you may find it unnerving when you hear your attorney giving her the chance to state all the reasons why you don't deserve custody. It is a much better idea to get those reasons out in the open now than have one or more of them emerge during the trial.

Have your attorney ask if the spouse has anything else to add

At the end of almost every deposition, I ask, "Is there anything else you want to tell me?" If your spouse's lawyer is good, he may object and direct her not to answer that open-ended question, but you probably have a better-than-even chance that the lawyer isn't very good and will allow her to answer. In fact, this is just the sort of question that obsessed and angry people love to answer. They have sat through two hours of questions waiting for their moment to unload all their invective on the record. When they do, they often say things that can hurt them in court. I have seen some people go on for five minutes or longer raving about a spouse's affair or his cheapness. Not only does their raving often characterize them as unstable, but they often make charges that simply aren't true or provable in court.

THE EXPERTS

The range of experts you may need can run the gamut, from accountants to psychologists to real-estate professionals. Beyond that, you may require highly specialized experts such as forensic accountants or psychologists who are proficient in a particular area, such as bipolar disorder (and know how someone with this disorder might function as a parent). Sometimes you must hire an expert to attempt to counter your spouse's expert's testimony. Sometimes you must find an expert when you suspect your spouse is hiding money or when there is a complex group of assets that need to be valued. In addition, courts appoint experts, usually for the purpose of custody evaluations, and their recommendations can have a huge and not always fair impact on custody decisions.

While every case is different, I can provide you with some guidelines that should serve you well, especially if your spouse is being unreasonable and experts can be a critical part of a court case:

Make sure the expert you hire has the right expertise for your divorce issues

This may seem obvious, but many times divorce attorneys rely on a small group of experts for all their cases. To a certain extent this makes sense, since for 75 percent of the cases they handle, these experts will be fine. In difficult cases, however, a more specialized expert may be required. I have had more than one case in which a spouse was hiding money outside this country through sophisticated estate planning and creditor protection devices. To uncover these schemes and offer credible, understandable court testimony, you need an expert who knows his stuff. Similarly, some retirement plans and their assets are so extensive and complicated that a garden-variety actuary may not be able to make heads or tails of them—or he may not be able to translate what he knows into language that your attorney or the court understands.

Don't let your attorney convince you that you'll be fine without experts

This may be true in cases that aren't all-out wars, but when there's a court battle looming and your spouse is vengeful, abusive, or irrational, an expert is often necessary. Some attorneys believe they have handled so many cases and seen so many different situations that nothing can surprise them. They're convinced that they can present a credible case without relying on expert testimony. They often make convincing arguments to their clients that experts cost money and so they should save their dollars and let the attorney take care of these complex issues. Don't be penny wise and pound foolish.

No doubt, sometimes the attorney can handle the case competently. If I were the client, however, and a custody decision or my retirement money were on the line, I would want an expert helping me state my case. Remember, too, that if the other side has an expert in a given area and you don't, you're at a disadvantage. In difficult cases, you can usually count on the other side using experts.

Find experts who can speak clearly, calmly, and convincingly

Some experts may have sterling credentials but when they get up in court to testify come across as biased, indecisive, confused, or incompetent. One psychologist was an expert witness for a mother who wanted to deny visitation to our firm's clients, who were the child's paternal grandparents. In this doctor's deposition, he claimed that the mother was a great parent who was rational, kind, and responsible. When we presented him with evidence that this same mom had accused these grandparents of devil worship, that she claimed they were in league with the devil and had raped her and delivered Satan's child, and that her accusations were actually taken from a famous movie, he became nonplussed and appeared uncertain and confused about his opinion of the mom. Obviously, this psychologist was not perceptive, which was fortunate for our clients. We received visitation rights for the grandparents shortly thereafter.

Don't use your treating therapist as an expert witness

There are four problems with this strategy. First, the therapist may appear to the judge as biased—he has probably been seeing you for a significant period of time and has a vested interested in communicating that he's helped you become a rational, psychologically sound human being. Second, many therapists have never appeared in court before and aren't used to being questioned aggressively about their conclusions by a skilled attorney. As a result, they become flustered and less than convincing. Third, when your therapist testifies in court, you may waive your highly confidential doctor-patient privilege, and you can expect the opposing attorney to ask questions about your psychological state and past behaviors that you probably prefer remain private. Fourth, you may find it difficult to continue seeing this therapist after he testifies in court—the testimony can affect how you view him and how he views you—and if you value him as a therapist, you may not want to jeopardize this relationship.

It is usually much better to find an independent therapist who has experience testifying in divorce court, who can examine a person objectively and render a clear and compelling opinion on the stand.

Make sure your attorney does her homework regarding court-appointed custody evaluators

Contrary to expectations, not all court-appointed custody evaluators are unbiased and insightful. Some enter the process with a clear (if sometimes unconscious) bias toward the mom or the dad. Some strongly believe that both parents should participate in the child-raising process in almost all but the most extreme instances, while others strongly believe that one parent should handle these tasks exclusively. Custody evaluators—who often are child psychiatrists, psychologists, or social workers—are by no means perfect and can make mistakes.

If your lawyer is smart and experienced, she should know most of the court-appointed evaluators in your area well. She should know that one custody evaluator resists recommending joint custody when the dad has a high-powered job that demands he work ten-hour days six days a week. She should be aware that another evaluator frequently recommends supervised visitation when dads have anger management problems and when their spouses express concern about these problems.

Knowing these patterns allows your attorney to adjust her legal strategy accordingly. Sometimes it helps your lawyer adjust her nonlegal strategy as well. One psychologist in Cook County was often appointed by a particular judge. This judge thought he was terrific, and she responded angrily whenever an attorney would question him aggressively in her courtroom. In one case, this psychologist had done a negative evaluation of my client, and I feared that it would hurt his chances of gaining joint custody. I also knew that I would have very little leeway to challenge his report in court. Fortunately, I was also aware that this psychologist had a reputation for being fickle. Before the trial, I took him out to dinner and went through the report with him, explaining exactly where I thought it was off. I didn't attempt to browbeat him or convince him to change his mind; I just pointed out specific facts that contradicted his report's conclusions. When he appeared in court, his testimony admitted the possible mistakes in his report and suggested that other, more positive conclusions about my client's fitness as a parent were warranted. The judge awarded my client joint custody.

CUSTODY CONSIDERATIONS
AND COMPLICATIONS

I f you want sole custody and your spouse wants to deny you custody, you need to be prepared for a war. Even if the issue is less serious—you both agree your spouse should have custody but you want a great deal of visitation—it can still become a war. In certain circumstances, custody battles are lost before they've begun. If you have a history of abusing your spouse or your kids, you probably will never be granted custody or even unsupervised visitation. If you abuse drugs and are sexually promiscuous and your spouse is a responsible parent, it's doubtful that a judge will grant you sole custody even if you're a good mom. Your lawyer should tell you right from the start if your custody goals are unrealistic.

Many times, though, your goals are reasonable. Ultimately, you need to convince the judge of their reasonableness. What can go a long way toward doing so is saying and doing the right things in the presence of the custody evaluator. During the evaluation, you're going to be asked a lot of questions about your relationship with your child as well as your relationship with your spouse. Here are some dos and don'ts regarding these questions:

Do:
- Be honest about your strengths and weaknesses as a parent; the evaluator will be watching for statements that contradict what he knows through his research to be true.

- Relate specific incidents involving your child that reflect that you spend quality time with her; name places, dates, and events that clearly demonstrate you enjoy a mutually enriching relationship.

- Express concern for your child's economic, emotional, and psychological welfare; communicate how you will attempt to establish a relationship with your ex-spouse after the divorce that will help rather than hurt your child.

Don't:
- Complain about things that your spouse did as a parent or accuse him of various "crimes" he never committed. If the evaluator asks you what type of parent you believe your spouse to be, be fair and focus on his positive qualities (assuming some exist). Obviously, if your spouse has a documented problem such as having served time in jail or being physically abusive, you can express concern about these issues. Do not, however, use the question as an opportunity to rant against your spouse's lack of interest in his kids or the criticism he regularly directs toward them.

- Act as if you don't have a clue when the evaluator asks you about your plans if you gain sole or joint custody. Have specific ideas about how you'll balance your work and parenting duties, where the kids will sleep when they stay with you, what you'll do with them, what school activities you'll go to, etc.

- Lose control. Don't lose your temper when the evaluator asks you a touchy question or start lecturing about how your gender gets the short end of the stick in most divorces.

Be passionate and committed about parenting, but remain calm and logical.

The evaluator may want to observe you interacting with your children. If so, play or converse with them as you normally would. Don't try and smother them with love, questions, or lectures. Be yourself. Demonstrate that you have a good relationship and that you feel comfortable interacting with your children and they feel comfortable interacting with you. If you appear disinterested or uncomfortable during these interactions—or, even worse, if you seem impatient or angry—this can work against you in the evaluation.

I should point out that the custody evaluation isn't necessarily binding. Your lawyer can challenge it if it's unfavorable, but you need solid grounds to challenge it. Typically, four grounds exist for challenges:

- **Clear bias.** For example, you may have examined the evaluator's recommendations in the last 30 cases in which he was involved and found that in 29 out of 30, he recommended sole custody for the father.

- **Poor credentials.** An example would be a psychological evaluator who isn't a licensed psychologist or has serious blemishes on his record, such as malpractice suits or professional disciplinary matters.

- **A lack of diligence.** Perhaps the evaluator spent only 10 minutes interviewing you and little or no time observing you with your children. As a result, his report is based on very sketchy information.

- **Incompetent evaluation.** This is probably the most difficult factor to demonstrate, but if the evaluator draws conclusions that have no basis in specific facts in his report—for example, he concludes you shouldn't have custody because you are an airplane pilot and never at home, while in reality you quit that job five years ago and are a stay-at-home dad—then it's possible to use this as the basis of a challenge.

Depending on the state in which you live or the particular situation you're in, other factors may enter into a custody decision. A social services home study investigation may be conducted and interviews with children may also take place. The big additional factor in fight-plagued divorces, however, is the appointment of a guardian ad litem (usually a lawyer) or an attorney for the child. This individual may serve as the children's advocate in a custody dispute. This advocacy can take many forms, depending on the appointment designation.

For instance, a Report of the Chicago Bar Association's Matrimonial Law Committee's Subcommittee on Attorney for Child/Guardian Ad Litem found the following:

- An attorney for the child is obligated to be an advocate for the child, but this is optional for a guardian ad litem.

- An attorney for the child cannot testify or file a report with the court, but a guardian ad litem can do both.

- An attorney for the child cannot advise the court at trial, but a guardian ad litem can do so.

Many times, guardian ad litems or attorneys for children are appointed because the parents are so consumed with hatred for each other that they are clearly neglecting the best interests of their kids. They may be engaging in horrific verbal and even physical battles in front of the kids; they may be making threats in front of the children or using them as pawns ("You're never going to see Jimmy again unless you give me the money you owe me!").

If an attorney for the child is appointed in your divorce case, do not deal with her directly unless your attorney consents. Rely on your attorney to help you when you need to communicate with the attorney or guardian. Above all else, calm down and do not turn your children into victims, since that's why she possibly became involved in the first place.

PRIVATE INVESTIGATORS: WHEN ORDINARY DISCOVERY FALLS SHORT

Your spouse may be cruel or crazy, but to the naked eye, he appears like a normal human being. Nothing in the official records indicates that he is likely to kidnap the children or be a deadbeat dad. He has never been hospitalized for his depression, and no one but you knows about his many affairs. If you rely on ordinary means to make a case for his likely bad conduct to the court, you'll probably lose.

A private investigator, though, can gather evidence of your spouse's immoral or illegal behavior in ways regular methods can't. He can dig through trash cans to find documentation of financial chicanery, and he can videotape your spouse buying drugs or bringing one sexual partner after another home when the kids are around. Using everything from the naked eye to sophisticated surveillance equipment, he can create a record of behavior that can be crucial in court.

Consider our three categories of difficult spouses and the types of information private investigators uncover about them:

Financially Difficult

- Accurate witness evidence of your spouse arranging to hide assets; conversations with brokers, friends, and family members asking them to participate in the scheme.

- Paperwork found in trash cans or obtained lawfully via computer technology offering evidence of financial schemes.

- Photographic evidence of your spouse handing cash to a co-conspirator for safekeeping.

Abusively Difficult

- Photographs or videotape of your spouse striking your child.

- Audiotapes of your spouse being verbally abusive (not just once, but exhibiting a consistently abusive pattern of behavior) authorized by a court order (if necessary).

- Finding witnesses who will testify to your spouse being physically or verbally abusive to you or the children.

Vengefully Difficult

- Uncovering a paper trail (purchased airline tickets, a residence in a foreign country, transfer of money offshore) revealing your spouse's scheme to flee the country after the trial and not pay you a dime of support.

- Finding a witness who will testify that your spouse intends to make you suffer by falsely accusing you of child abuse.

- Making a case through taped conversations if allowed by court order to protect kids, and intercepted e-mails or other evidence that your spouse is plotting to kidnap your children or force you into bankruptcy once the trial is finished.

In one case, Jerry was the owner of a local retail chain of hardware stores. He was financially well off, and when he decided to divorce Marcia, he was fine with her request for sole custody and was perfectly willing to make child support payments based on his income. Marcia, however, suspected that he had been grossly understating his income in recent years, perhaps in order to avoid paying her the amount of child support due her. Marcia's lawyer hired a private investigator who followed her spouse for a week, and during that time saw him hand a large envelope containing cash to one of his store managers. Though the retail chain wasn't exclusively a cash business, a great deal of money did exchange hands in each of the stores. The investigator began interviewing the various store managers and one of them finally admitted that Jerry had been funneling cash to each of them in order to reduce his income, and that he had concocted a scheme to "recirculate" the money back to him after the divorce was final. Because Marcia didn't want Jerry to end up in jail, where he couldn't support anyone, she insisted only that he report his correct income to the IRS, which he did. And of course, she wanted to receive the legally correct amount of child support, which Jerry also agreed to give her.

Many times, of course, the investigator's revelations don't automatically result in an immediate settlement favorable to his client. Nonetheless, the information he gathers may be useful in court, even if it is limited to the investigator's observations.

If you need to use a private investigator, your lawyer will probably recommend someone she's worked with in the past and believes is good. Though you'll probably have to take her word that this person is good, you should ask your lawyer the following questions before she brings him onto your team:

- Does the investigator have a good reputation? Was he a well-respected police officer before becoming a P.I.? How long has he been an investigator, and how many similar types of divorce cases has he worked on? Has he ever been in jail or been the subject of negative publicity? Is he able to speak clearly and intelligently, and will he present himself well on the stand?

- Is the P.I. going to receive a clear set of instructions? Can you point him in a specific direction and tell him what he's trying to discover? Do you feel that a P.I. can uncover the behavior or the plans the spouse is trying to hide better than any other form of discovery?

In terms of the first bullet point, if your P.I. has a bad reputation, the judge will probably be aware of it and discount whatever evidence he uncovers or testimony he offers.

In terms of the second point, remember that private investigators aren't always the best option. It may be that you can check out your suspicions about your spouse in some other way, or that you lack any real knowledge about any wrongdoing. The worst thing you can do is tell a P.I. to "look for something, anything we can use in court." This overly general instruction usually results in worthless information.

Remember, too, that your lawyer should hire the investigator. This way, if the investigation goes sour, it may not be subject to the opposing attorney's discovery requests because it will likely be considered your attorney's work product.

THE TRIAL: WINNING VERSUS LOSING

In most instances, neither your attorney, your spouse's attorney, nor the overworked judge wants your divorce case to go to trial. In the weeks or months preceding the trial date, your attorney will probably suggest or discuss settlement options with you. The judge may urge settlement upon both you and your spouse in a pretrial hearing. However, if both you and your spouse refuse to budge, you will have your day in court.

It may be that this is the day your vengeful spouse has longed for, and he wants nothing more than to air his grievances against you in public. He may not care about the expense or the stress of a trial; he simply wants to place your alleged offenses against him on the public record. If this describes your spouse, then you can expect a nasty courtroom battle in which he may call your friends, neighbors, and work colleagues as witnesses, not necessarily to make his case against you, but to humiliate you.

No matter how awful your spouse is acting, however, you need to maintain your cool and focus on the good reasons why you're going to trial: to gain the custody you deserve, to protect your children's financial future, to keep your inheritance, to protect your kids against an abusive spouse, and so on.

I've found it also helps clients to know in advance how a trial might unfold, since a divorce war in court can involve all sorts of unpleasant events. Familiarity with how the legal process works can make it a bit more tolerable. Therefore, here is the chronology of a divorce trial and the unpleasant things that occur in each stage:

1. **Both sides "maneuver" before the trial even begins.** There are pretrial motions and conferences, discussions of ground rules, and other strategic and informational-related actions. Even when the trial actually starts, it can become a start-and-stop process, with recesses mandated by the unavailability of an expert witness at a given time or conflicts in the judge's schedule. You're probably anxious and raring to go to trial, but you must recognize that because your case is so contentious, a lot of maneuvering on the part of both attorneys is par for the course. Trust your lawyer when he tells you that the delays and pretrial conferences are important to building your case, unless you're absolutely convinced that something else is going on (in which case you should quickly find another lawyer to obtain a second opinion).

2. **Each attorney makes an opening statement.** Listening to your spouse's attorney's statement may be tough to take, since your lawyer probably won't object to it or respond in any way until it's time for his statement. No doubt, the opposing attorney will claim he will present evidence that you are a neglectful parent, a tightwad, abusive, an alcoholic, or guilty of whatever bad behavior your spouse feels

you've committed. The good news is that your spouse's attorney may be making wild charges that won't be supported by the evidence. For instance, just because you have a bad temper doesn't mean the opposing attorney will be able to present evidence establishing you are an abusive parent if there is no evidence of abuse.

3. **The plaintiff or petitioner presents his side first.** If your spouse is the plaintiff, his lawyer will present documentary evidence (written records, videos, etc.) and put their witnesses on the stand for direct testimony (you may even be called as an adverse witness). Your attorney can cross-examine these witnesses when they've finished. Your spouse's lawyer can then redirect questions, and your attorney can engage in recross after redirect. To deal effectively with this part of the trial, maintain an involved but controlled attitude. If you hear a witness say something that you know is false, you should write a note to your attorney telling her about it; if you feel it's an urgent matter that can make your case, relay this to your attorney, who may request a recess to discuss it with you. Under no circumstances, however, should you lose control. Don't play to the judge by shaking your head constantly when your spouse's witnesses testify or shouting at your attorney that "you shouldn't let him get away with that!" Your displays of outrage and anger may be justified, but they likely will have a negative impact on the judge.

4. **The defendant or respondent presents her case.** The same process as in the previous point is followed. Again, don't act out. You're not going to like the charges made against you, but keep a straight face.

5. **Your attorney and opposing counsel make closing arguments.** Many times, however, the judge does not render a decision immediately after these statements. In complex cases, such as those involving custody, it may take weeks until he makes his decision.

Many factors influence the outcome of the trial, from the credentials and testimony of your expert witnesses to hard evidence about your or your spouse's behavior (such as arrests, drug or alcohol problems, or psychological disorders). Sometimes, a judge's predilections (he may be pro-mom or pro-dad) determine the outcome. Sometimes, the laws of certain states have an impact (some states have minimum child support guidelines based on the noncustodial parent's net income, while other states base it on gross income). Obviously, the work your lawyer has done before the trial has a major bearing on the outcome.

Contrary to myth, children usually don't testify during trials. Evidence from a custody evaluator (who has met with them) or an in camera (in chambers) conference with the judge (who interviewed them) may have an impact, but it's relatively rare to have a television moment when a child testifies and says dramatically, "I want to live with Mommy (or Daddy)."

During the trial, however, you may take the stand, and what you have to say can affect the judge's decision. Here are some tips in this regard:

- **Do not testify if you don't believe you can control yourself.** When I have an angry client (who may be angry for very good reasons) who insists on testifying, I'll often have him see a mental health professional prior to taking the stand. Even if the client is not angry, I'll take the time to prepare him for the types of questions he can expect from the opposing attorney. Some of these questions can be tough: "Did you tell your friend, Jane, that you hoped the divorce trial would bankrupt your spouse?" Or: "On the night of December fourth, did you state in Al's Bar that you would rather burn down the house than allow your wife to have it?"

- **Express your concerns rather than place blame.** Your instinct will be to tell your story, to reveal to the judge why your cause is just and why your spouse is a liar, a cheat, and a hundred other bad things. Don't listen to your instinct. Instead, listen to your attorney, who, if she's good, will instruct you to let others, such as expert witnesses, place blame on your spouse. In response to friendly questions from your attorney or antagonistic ones from the opposing lawyer, focus on your concerns about specific incidents. Don't accuse your spouse of being an uninvolved parent when your attorney asks you about his unwillingness to go to your children's parent-teacher conferences. Instead, say you were concerned that he missed eight straight conferences in a row. If you come across to the judge as vindictive or abusive or aberrant in any way, she will probably be skeptical of what you have to say.

- **Focus on your relationship with your child during testimony rather than your spouse's relationship with the child.** As you're asked questions, your responses should convey to the judge specific experiences involving yourself and your child that display an emotional bond. By communicating all the things you do together and how much pleasure you both take in these activities, you make a stronger case for your custody or visitation requests. While you may suggest concern about specific incidents involving your spouse and your child, you should not resort to name-calling or paranoid accusations during your testimony.

HOW TO GIVE YOURSELF AN EDGE

As I've indicated, divorce trial outcomes can turn on factors out of your control or be based on irrefutable evidence about your marital estate, your finances, your past behavior, and so on. Still, besides the advice offered earlier, you can give yourself an edge in ugly divorces by following the following "rules."

First, if you want joint or sole custody, consider changing behaviors that the court may look on negatively. For instance, you may want to consider decreasing your work hours if you work 50 or more hours weekly. Our firm had a client, a very wealthy doctor, who routinely worked over 70 hours a week. He wanted sole custody, and he had a good argument for it because there was ample evidence that his wife was dependent on a variety of prescription drugs and was a neglectful mom. Nonetheless, the court was unlikely to award custody to our client unless he decreased his work hours. Fortunately, he did so, resigning from his practice and finding a position that required much less of his time. He was awarded sole custody. Similarly, if you're fighting for support payments and claiming you require more than your spouse wants to pay or the state-mandated percentage, you may want to show the court that you are not spending money on frivolous purchases. You might drop your membership in an exclusive country club, stop going to day spas a few times a week, and stop making large purchases of jewelry and clothing.

Second, maintain the boundaries your lawyer establishes. One boundary concerns your interactions with your spouse prior to and during the trial. You should not engage in public screaming matches with him, threaten him, dump all his possessions on the lawn, or withhold money rightfully due him or the kids. Another boundary is with your lawyer. She is not your friend. You should not attempt to establish a social relationship with her. Her effectiveness is predicated on her objectivity. If she becomes your friend, she may not have the detachment necessary to act in your best interests. I've known more than one lawyer who became so involved with their clients and so angry at what their clients' spouses were doing to them that they insisted on a fight to the death—a trial with a clear winner and loser. If they had been more objective, they might have tried to settle the cases, resulting in a better outcome for their clients.

Third, refuse to fall under the influence of outsiders. Your friends, family, and work colleagues are all going to offer you advice about how you can win your divorce trial. At best this advice is well-meaning but wrong-headed; at worst, it will cause you to lose your trial. I had one client who became a member of a men's support group whose members were very angry and anti-women (good men's support groups exist, but this wasn't one of them). Though I strongly urged him to avoid this group, he was adamant about remaining a member. As a result, he behaved abysmally toward his wife before and during the trial, acting paranoid during his court testimony and using profanity when describing her. During a lunch break when the court wasn't in session, he drove his pickup truck around the court building with an effigy of the judge hanging in the back while yelling into a bullhorn that the judge should be kicked off the bench. It wasn't surprising that the judge's ruling went against him.

Ideally, these three actions will give you a bit of an edge and result in a favorable verdict. However, whatever the outcome, the trial may not be the end of the process. Ugly divorces have a much higher percentage of evolving into post-divorce actions than relatively normal ones. Let's look at what you need to know in order to deal with a nasty case after the trial is done or a settlement has been reached.

CHAPTER SEVEN

Post-Decree Strategy: The Divorce Is Done but Your Ex-Spouse Isn't

A divorce is never over, especially when the divorce has been a war. Many people breathe a great sigh of relief when a settlement is agreed to or a judgment is rendered, but these events don't necessarily signal the end of either litigation or feuding. In fact, many people are asking for trouble when they let their guard down. They assume everything has been settled and then do or say something that ignites a costly, stressful series of post-decree actions. Or they may do nothing to catalyze these actions but are unprepared when their ex-spouse asks the court to reduce child support payments or files a petition to move out of state with the kids.

Many clients tell me that post-decree fighting is even worse than pre-decree for three reasons. First, psychologically, people have it set in their mind that a difficult phase of their life has finally ended, and so they become extremely upset when they realize that this difficult period had only a superficial ending. Second, the battles after the divorce is "final" often are fiercer and involve more emotionally charged issues than before. Third, post-divorce reality sinks in and people feel like they got the short end of the stick. The custodial parent may believe that she didn't receive a fair financial settlement but received all the responsibility while her ex-spouse is off having the time of his life; the noncustodial parent may resent seeing his children infrequently, believe his ex-spouse is poisoning their minds against him, and feel he is paying far too much support for too little time with his kids.

While you can't prevent your ex-spouse from trying to make your life a living hell after the divorce, you can decrease the odds substantially that the divorce war will continue or erupt anew. To achieve this goal, we need to look at the most common post-decree legal actions and how to deal with them in the most effective manner possible.

First, though, let's look at the typical catalysts for these legal actions and what you can do to avoid triggering them.

HOW TO AVOID RESTARTING
THE DIVORCE WAR

You may not want to continue the battle with your spouse after you're divorced, but you may find yourself inadvertently doing something that enrages him or makes him feel that you're a selfish, manipulative jerk. It's not always possible to avoid the catalysts that cause people to file motions and countermotions and become embroiled in post-divorce litigation. Still, you may minimize problems if you avoid the following mistakes:

Getting remarried right away

If you remarry within a year or so after the divorce, expect your spouse to blow a fuse, especially if she has not remarried. People frequently harbor hope of getting back together with their spouse, despite the reality of the divorce and all the difficulty they experienced during their marriage. Similarly, if you remarry quickly, it's like sending a message to your spouse that you're going to be in a happy, rewarding relationship for the rest of your life while she will be miserable and alone. None of this is necessarily true, but when the wounds of a bad marriage and an argument-filled divorce are still fresh, remarriage can cause your spouse to try to obtain her pound of flesh.

In addition, one of the most common triggers for post-decree litigation involves stepparents who assume roles traditionally reserved for biological parents. At the most extreme, they may physically discipline their stepchild; they may also verbally berate that child, or simply impose discipline such as forbidding the child from playing sports until his grades improve. Your ex-spouse may feel threatened and believe your new spouse has crossed the line by trying to take over her parenting role. She may respond by filing a motion claiming that the stepparent's actions are harming the child physically or psychologically. In the worst-case scenario, this motion can lead to the start of a new custody trial.

For this reason, set parenting boundaries with your new spouse. Clearly, these boundaries can be tough to observe in complex parenting situations, but it may help if you agree that certain types of discipline can be administered only by you or your ex-spouse.

Ideally, of course, you both will quickly find new partners and remarry, in which case remarriage probably won't be a catalyst for post-decree litigation. But if you're the only one remarrying, expect problems. To avoid them, consider delaying the remarriage. Recognize that your ex is likely to respond irrationally; she may demand more child support or try to gain full custody of your children. Most of the time, the arguments for a change in terms are specious and won't stand up in court. Nonetheless, the fresh legal actions can make your life a living hell until they're resolved.

Similarly, if you start seeing someone regularly or move in with her, this can also act as a catalyst even without a formal engagement or marriage. Obviously, if your new partner exhibits behaviors that are detrimental to your kids, your spouse has a legitimate reason to seek legal redress. Most of the time, though, it will be the mere existence of this partner that will set off your ex-spouse. Therefore, be discreet. Try and limit your kids' exposure to this new person in your life for at least a year after the divorce. Remember that if you find someone and your ex-spouse has no one, it may evoke strong negative emotions that eventually can translate into legal action.

Moving to another city or state

If you're the custodial parent and decide to move, you should understand that even expressing a desire to do so—let alone filing a removal petition with the court—will probably make your ex-spouse furious. This is not something you should undertake lightly. You shouldn't move simply because you have always wanted to live in California, or because you met someone you like who lives in another city or state.

For some noncustodial moms and dads, your intent to move is nothing less than a declaration of war. It sends a message that they will no longer enjoy the same relationship with their children that they enjoyed in the past; that the greater distance between them and their kids will make it impossible to see them as often as in the past.

Expect the noncustodial spouse to fight back with everything he has. He is unlikely to allow you to make this move without protest, and he may not fight fair. Expect him to raise best-interest-of-the-child arguments, threaten to file a motion to reduce support (if you're moving in with another person who has significant income), or even try to challenge your fitness as a parent.

If you have a legitimate reason to move—say, both you and your spouse are unemployed and barely getting by and you receive a good job offer that will allow your child to attend a better school—then you may have a case to make and it may be worth the fight. If you're moving for a reason that has nothing to do with the best interest of your child, however, you may be better off postponing the move until your kids are older and the dust from the divorce has settled. At the very least, you should think long and hard about how you might make the move acceptable to your ex-spouse before doing anything about it. Perhaps you can discuss it with him and suggest a plan whereby he gets to take the kids for a month or more during the summer, or offer some alternative that will make him more amenable to the move. Introducing the "possibility" of moving in conversation will help you measure his reaction. If he blows his stack at even the possibility, you may want to defer the move to a later time.

Failing to make child support or other payments mandated by the court

Don't expect your ex-spouse to let you slide, no matter what your reasoning—being fired from a job, becoming ill, or some other misfortune. Nonetheless, many people expect exactly this; they assume that their former partner will understand the spot they're in. As a result, they reduce their payments or stop them entirely without legal protection.

If you're experiencing financial problems and can't make your payments, you need to request a reduction or abatement by the court. If you don't, your ex-spouse will likely take advantage of the legal system and you'll be back in court facing not only back payments but legal bills and possible incarceration.

Gaining a lot of money but refusing to discuss an increase or decrease of support

It doesn't matter whether you win the lottery, receive a huge promotion, inherit a fortune, or remarry a millionaire—these positive changes in your financial circumstances can cause your ex-spouse to demand more support or request that his financial obligation to you be reduced. Of course, your ex-spouse needs to know about these events before he reacts, and it's much better if the news comes from you than from some other source. When he learns about it secondhand and considerably after the fact, he'll feel like you've been hiding this information and be angry.

In some instances, you are bound by your divorce agreement to reveal these events within a specific time period, and you can expect whatever financial agreement you have to be affected accordingly.

It is much better if you both can deal with these issues in a civil manner and reach an equitable revision of your arrangement on your own. As a general rule of thumb, however, this equitable revision is less likely to occur if (a) the amount of money you come into is large; (b) you hide the news from your ex-spouse and he finds out from a third party; or (c) your relationship since the divorce has gone from bad to worse and your ex-spouse is just looking for a reason to take you back to court.

Failing to adhere to the terms of a visitation agreement

If you want to antagonize your ex-spouse to the point that he files post-decree motions, ignore the visitation agreement. Bring your children home hours after you're supposed to, or instead of bringing them home on Sunday after a weekend visit, extend the weekend for a few days by taking them to Disney World or some other fun spot, causing them to miss school. If you're the custodial parent, you may make excuses about why your kids can't visit on designated days or why the visits need to be cut short. You may also decide that you're going to be present the entire time that your ex-spouse is with your kids, conveying that you don't trust him. No matter how you rationalize or justify these actions, they invariably will create difficulties between you and your spouse that often lead to additional legal battles.

I recognize that there are times when it's impossible to adhere to visitation terms, but you should make these exceptions rather than rule. If you are going to keep your child a few additional hours, clear it with your ex-spouse in advance, or at least before the few additional hours have passed by. There are also going to be times when you have a special event to which you want to take your kids and your spouse has a different event. Don't arbitrarily violate the agreement terms just because you believe your event is more important. Instead, negotiate. Trade one visitation day in the future for an extra visitation day this weekend.

Spending money seemingly beyond your means

Though you can barely make your child support payment and complain bitterly to your ex-spouse about the financial pressure you're under, you buy your child a car for her sixteenth birthday. Or, if you're the one receiving support and are constantly asking your ex for more money to help you make ends meet, you take the kids on a European vacation. Or you buy a beach home. Or you mention that you just bought a boat.

If your spouse believes that you're spending excessive amounts of money, he may suspect that you're holding out on him—that you have a hidden cache of money or a secret source of income, or perhaps that you're taking money out of your kids' college savings account. It may be that you have a legitimate source for the money you're spending and your ex-spouse is jealous or thinks you're spending more than you are. Whatever the reason, he may have his lawyer file a post-decree motion demanding his payments be reduced given your "obvious" lavish lifestyle.

Rather than antagonize your ex-spouse and prolong the divorce battle, be open and honest with him about your spending. Tell him if you took out a loan to make a purchase or if your new boyfriend paid for the European vacation.

Sometimes the things that anger ex-spouses post-decree may seem innocuous. You may say or do something that seems trivial—you mention that you really like the new car she purchased, for example—yet she thinks you're scheming to reduce your support payments and decides to strike first and go after you for more money. Clearly, if your spouse is vengeful, money-crazed, or abusive, you may not have to do much to prompt her to prolong the divorce battle past the settlement or court judgment. All you can do is be aware of what sets your ex-spouse off and do everything possible to steer clear of those subjects.

If your spouse is a truly difficult person, her post-decree strikes may be capricious and have nothing to do with your actions. She may suddenly get it into her head to take the kids and move to another state without informing either you or the court. Or she may charge you with abuse for no reason other than that she doesn't like you and wants to find a way to cut you out of your child's life. Sometimes, no cause and effect exists regarding these types of post-decree behaviors, and all you can do is be aware that your ex-spouse remains on the warpath and is capable of all types of egregious moves. You need to take any threat seriously—even if she tells you she's going to run away with the kids to her old boyfriend's house in Japan unless you give her more money—and inform your lawyer of the threat and discuss what you might do to prevent it.

THE POST-DECREE PROCESS:
WHAT YOU CAN EXPECT

Before we examine the best strategies to handle post-decree actions, you need to understand a bit about the process. This will help you know what you can and cannot do after the divorce is final, whether your spouse initiates actions against you or you're the one seeking redress.

First, be aware that most courts are reluctant to change the essence of a divorce decree or settlement unless a legal basis for doing so exists. The reasoning is that you need to test out the agreement over a period of time to determine its viability. As a result, if you file a motion for additional child support after the divorce, the courts will probably not give you the additional money you request unless a substantial change in circumstances occurs that merits the change. For instance, if you or your spouse is fired or one of you is convicted for selling drugs and is incarcerated, the court will be willing to hear your argument. Therefore, before filing anything, consider whether you have the correct legal basis for doing so.

The legal basis can vary considerably depending on circumstances. For instance, let's say you agreed to give your spouse custody and decide six months later that doing so was not in the best interest of the child. Unless you have extremely compelling evidence to back up this belief, the court probably won't entertain this petition. In most jurisdictions, you must wait at least two years to change a custody agreement unless there is proof of child endangerment. On the other hand, if it's not a custody matter, you may be able to access post-decree court immediately. For instance, let's say that after six months, you discover that your spouse concealed marital assets. Therefore, you can enter a pleading that your divorce agreement was based on fraud or misrepresentation. If you have solid proof of this fraud, the court is likely to set aside the basis for the agreement.

Second, be aware that mediation is usually mandated in many divorce settlements for problems that arise post-divorce. This is especially true for custody and visitation issues. Rather than go directly to court, a mediator is appointed for dispute resolution. In fact, you should make sure your settlement contains a mediation clause. In some instances, the court will appoint a mediator. If your particular jurisdiction doesn't provide a court-appointed mediator, you and your ex-spouse should find someone who is competent to referee whatever disputes arise post-decree and name this person in the mediation clause of your agreement. In Illinois and many other states, just about anyone can call himself a mediator. You should find someone who at least has taken courses in mediation, has years of experience as a mediator, and who is recommended by your lawyer or other professionals.

Third, in most instances, neither you nor your ex-spouse can move without filing a removal petition that demonstrates the move is in the best interest of the child. Your agreement probably stipulates that the custodial parent cannot move without filing a petition for removal with the court. Even if it doesn't, however, don't expect the court to allow you to move just because you want to live in a better climate or have a lateral job offer from a company in another state. As I noted earlier, you must demonstrate the move will benefit your child in some way, such as better schools or a better standard of living because your new job will pay more.

Fourth, you need evidence of cause if you want to change some aspect of your divorce agreement; reports of suspicious behavior and vague statements won't suffice. For instance, suppose you believe that your spouse has bought a new condominium and a boat, but in the papers filed with the court he stated that his annual income is only $45,000. You put two and two together and demand that your attorney file a motion for increased or decreased support (depending on whether you're the custodial parent). Before your attorney does so, she will likely advise you about the time and costs involved in trying to prove that your suspicions are accurate—you may need to subpoena records, take depositions of accountants, and so on. You may want to go through an intermediary step in which you ask your ex-spouse to explain how he was able to afford the condo and boat. Maybe he has a good explanation. Maybe he didn't make these purchases. Or maybe he is willing to give you more money as soon as you bring up your suspicions. If his response satisfies you, you may avoid unnecessary legal costs and the slow-moving legal process.

Fifth, the legal quality of your agreement has a significant impact on what happens during the post-decree process. Some agreements are inflexible, vague, or incomplete—they don't mandate alternative dispute resolution in case of disagreements or offer an annual review of your agreement provisions concerning issues that change over time, such as custody, visitation, and support. Flexibility and specificity are two hallmarks of good agreements, especially when it comes to post-divorce issues. The best judgments for dissolution of marriage contain joint parenting provisions and support awards that are fair and include provisions for mediation if circumstances render the agreement less fair in the future. They often include financial penalties for unnecessary post-decree litigation—penalties in which the loser of the dispute must not only pay his own but his ex-spouse's attorney fees. If you have all these elements in your agreement, then it's likely you can resolve whatever issues come up without spending a great deal of time litigating a solution.

CUSTODY, VISITATION, AND SUPPORT: COMMON POST-DIVORCE DISPUTES AND WHAT TO DO ABOUT THEM

When you thought the divorce was over but either you or your ex-spouse challenges the divorce agreement, it can seem as if the process will drag on forever, and involve many more dollars and much more stress. My goal here is to provide you with some advice that will reduce the time, money, and stress involved in the post-decree process. Dividing the discussion into the three areas noted in this section's subtitle, I'm going to look at both the legal and practical context in which disputes take place.

Custody

You may have a joint custody arrangement and feel post-divorce events mandate that you should have sole custody. Or perhaps your spouse has sole custody but you believe circumstances dictate that you should have shared custody. In either case, you need to examine the situation carefully to determine whether you have grounds for filing a motion. Even if a court-appointed mediator provides free dispute resolution, it's still going to be a difficult process and should not be entered into lightly. Trying to change the custody agreement will probably infuriate your ex-spouse and make your relationship worse than before, and it may cause your children emotional harm. The situation may also be impossible for the mediator to resolve and you may end up back in court, where you'll be involved in a costly legal battle. Therefore, the first thing you need to do is determine whether you have grounds to challenge the agreement. Typically, courts are reluctant to make custody changes during the two-year period after the initial custody award unless there is a dramatic shift in circumstances demonstrating that the custodial parent is endangering the children in some way.

To help you determine whether you have a decent chance of challenging the agreement (or if your ex-spouse's challenge will be effective), place a check mark next to any of the following statements that apply to your situation:

❑ The children's primary residence has become that of the non-custodial parent.
❑ The kids spend half their time with each parent, even though one parent has sole custody.
❑ A stepparent is physically or verbally abusing a child or exhibiting other behaviors that are having a negative impact.
❑ The custodial parent has been convicted of a serious crime.
❑ There is clear evidence that the custodial parent is using illegal drugs or is an alcoholic.
❑ The custodial parent leaves younger kids alone for long periods of time.
❑ The custodial parent mistreats, causes, or ignores a child's medical problems.
❑ A therapist will testify that the custodial parent is emotionally unstable or has a particular condition that makes parenting difficult if not impossible.
❑ The custodial parent is sexually abusing the kids.

❑ The custodial parent has filed demonstrably false charges of sexual abuse against the noncustodial parent.

❑ The child is getting in serious trouble at school, failing courses, or exhibiting other major problems.

❑ The custodial parent is engaging in a systematic campaign to alienate the children from the noncustodial parent or preventing him from seeing his kids, and there is clear evidence of this campaign (letters, e-mails, conversations, witnesses who will testify in court).

❑ The custodial parent is endangering the children by having loaded weapons in the house that aren't under lock and key, lives in a high-crime neighborhood, or is in a house that is unsafe for other reasons (such as having a fire hazard).

Whether you're the custodial or noncustodial parent, you should also be aware that just placing a check mark next to one of these items doesn't mean you're certain to change custody terms. Obviously, the more evidence you have and the more egregious the behavior of the other parent, the more likely you'll achieve the custody modification you desire. Before engaging in a post-divorce battle over this issue, however, recognize that the odds of winning or losing are also affected by the following:

• The prevailing sentiment that all things being equal, the child should remain with the custodial parent. As a rule, judges don't like to change custody arrangements, because they believe that maintaining the status quo of the current arrangement provides stability for kids. Unless a parent has a strong case to modify a custody agreement (i.e., a child is clearly in danger under the current agreement), judges are reluctant to order a modification.

- A child is requesting a change in custody and has a credible reason for doing so. Judges are wary of younger children who say they want to be with Mommy or Daddy because that parent promised them something if they would say it. They also are wary of kids who are manipulative, playing one parent off against the other. If they argue that they want to stop living with Dad because his girlfriend hits them or they want joint custody because Mom works long hours and Dad could take care of them at least part of the time when she is working, these more credible arguments tend to carry more weight.

- The parent requesting custody modification should be able to provide evidence that not only is the other parent harming the kids in some way, but that he will be able to do a better job if granted joint or sole custody. In other words, the custodial parent may be neglectful, but if the noncustodial parent has a drinking problem, then few judges would transfer custody to him.

Visitation

To give you a sense of when the courts are more likely to modify visitation agreements, let me share two examples, the first involving a noncustodial parent and the second involving a custodial one.

Jack is a top executive with a Fortune 500 company, and his job is stressful and demanding. His wife, Jean, agreed to a generous visitation schedule that involved every weekend and one night per week plus the entire summer vacation. During the first two months after the divorce, Jack adhered to this schedule. After about a year, however, he began missing visits. Part of the problem was a more intense work schedule. Part of it, though, was his involvement with a woman who also had children, and this woman's expectation that he would be a father to her children (their biological father had supervised visitation). Despite Jean's requests that Jack show up when his kids were expecting him, he failed to do so. At first, she talked to him about how disappointed his seven-year-old daughter and nine-year-old son were when he had to cancel his visits—or even worse, when he didn't call to cancel them. Then she warned him that she wouldn't tolerate this behavior much longer. In his own mind, Jack rationalized his behavior, convincing himself that Jean just wanted to aggravate him and that he would go back to the visitation schedule when things calmed down at work and after his relationship with his new family stabilized.

Jean refused to wait until that time. Her attorney filed a petition with the court requesting a severe reduction in visitation, and she had gathered ample proof that Jack had consistently failed to show up for visits with his kids. The court granted the reduction.

The other example involves Lisa, the custodial mom of a five-year-old son, and her ex-husband, Tom. Lisa harbored a great deal of ill will toward Tom, whose affair with another woman precipitated the divorce. During the first three years after the divorce, Lisa generally complied with the visitation agreement, though sometimes she would call Tom and make excuses for why he couldn't come over on the designated day. Though this behavior irritated Tom and he didn't believe Lisa's excuses, it happened infrequently enough that he tolerated it. When Tom remarried three years after the divorce, however, things started getting worse. One month, Lisa forced Tom to miss half his scheduled visits. Even her excuses—their son wasn't feeling well, she had arranged a play date that conflicted with the visit—became less and less believable. Then, Lisa stopped calling with excuses; Tom would show up at the house to pick up his son to find no one home. Though Lisa never admitted to him that she was punishing him for his remarriage, Tom suspected that was her motive. She had told mutual friends that she resented that he was happy and she was not, and her only way to punish him was by preventing him from seeing his son.

Finally, Tom had had enough. When Lisa refused to listen to his pleas to let him resume his regular visitation schedule, he began documenting her "visitation abuse" and was able to convince their mutual friends to testify about their conversations with his ex-wife. Eventually, the court not only ordered her to maintain the visitation schedule mandated by their agreement and ordered her to pay all of Tom's legal fees and costs involved in his visitation enforcement action, but warned her that she would be incarcerated if she failed to maintain the schedule in the future.

In the first scenario, Jack made his wife miserable and caused his children to feel rejected after the divorce by failing to show up. In the second, Lisa used visitation as a weapon of revenge, causing her son to believe that his dad didn't love him. Both their ex-spouses gathered evidence of these behaviors and were able to use them to persuade the courts to provide stability for the children.

Now let's look at two lists. The first is a list of reasons the courts generally find unacceptable for modifying visitation arrangements. The second list includes situations and behaviors where the courts are more likely to modify these arrangements:

Unacceptable reasons for modification
- The noncustodial parent needs to change some visitation times because of social conflicts.

- The noncustodial parent's visits are "disruptive"—the kids are overly excited when this parent visits or takes them to his residence, and they have trouble falling asleep the first night they return home.

- The custodial parent hires a nanny or uses day care to watch her kids and prefers this arrangement to their being with the noncustodial parent.

- The custodial parent begins a serious relationship with another person and this person is a frequent visitor at the home.

Potentially acceptable reasons for modification

- Evidence of physical or sexual abuse by a parent.

- The custodial parent is guilty of "visitation abuse"— consistently prevents the noncustodial parent from seeing his child or ruins or shortens each visit.

- The noncustodial parent consistently fails to show up to take the child during scheduled visitation.

- Living conditions in the custodial parent's home are abysmal—for example, there is lack of food or regular, nutritious meals, or the home is filthy, overcrowded, or presents dangerous conditions.

Before embarking on a legal campaign to change visitation terms, understand that it's rare for the court to suspend or supervise a noncustodial parent's visitation privileges unless that parent poses a clear danger to the child. The court is much more likely to reduce visitation. It is equally rare for the court to enforce the non-custodial parent's visitation aggressively by incarceration or changing the visitation terms dramatically. Judges tend to issue "slap-on-the-wrist" warnings to custodial parents who cause their ex-spouses to miss an occasional visit, and they seldom expand visitation time because custodial parents have made a mistake in some way.

Still, legal action may be worthwhile, if for nothing else than a "shot across the bow" may somehow benefit the kids. Taking action shows your ex-spouse that you're serious about adhering to visitation terms, and it often gets results. If you want the court to modify your visitation agreement, be aware that you must be thorough and meticulous in your accumulation of evidence. You need to go beyond telling the court, "My wife deliberately made me miss three visitation days in the last six months," or "Every time my husband returns my child, she's upset and she told me he spanks her whenever she does something wrong." You must accumulate as much physical evidence as possible along with testimony of witnesses if you hope to gain a modification. To that end, here are some actions you should take:

- If you're the noncustodial parent, adhere to the visitation schedule religiously. If you miss dates and are constantly late, you may negate whatever visitation abuse is being committed by your ex-spouse. Your behavior may also cause her to commit the abuse in response to your tardiness.

- Try reasoning with your ex-spouse before you start preparing for a legal action. If your ex-spouse is a truly difficult person—if she's abusive to you and the kids or if she's bent on using the kids as a tool of vengeance—then talk won't do much good. On the other hand, I've had clients who were at each other's throats over visitation issues but found that if they calmed down and talked things out (or saw a therapist), they were able to put their child's welfare above their own grievances and accusations.

- If reasoning doesn't work, send a certified letter to your ex-spouse, informing her that you want to clarify the terms of your visitation and make sure that she understands these terms and will abide by them. Make sure your lawyer reads and approves the letter before you mail it.

- If your ex-spouse ignores this letter, you should have a witness to observe the offending behavior during visitation. Whether you're the custodial parent who needs to witness your ex's abusive behavior toward you or your kids or the noncustodial parent who needs a witness for how your ex consistently thwarts your attempts at visitation, corroboration of your charges is critical. Make sure you also keep written and/or videotaped records of everything that takes place.

- File a Petition for Enforcement of Parental Rights and other relief. A judge may send your ex-spouse a warning threatening punishment if the same violation occurs again, assess civil penalties, issue contempt of court citations, expand or reduce visitation, or even change custody terms in extreme cases.

Support

While all sorts of money-related disputes can arise post-decree, the most common one involves support payments. Generally, common sense prevails regarding petitions for review of support arrangements. If one parent suddenly has a big jump in income, the other parent may legitimately petition the court for increased payments. If one parent loses his job and experiences a sharp decline in income, he can petition the court for reduced payments with the expectation that his request will probably be granted.

Many times, however, the issues aren't clear-cut. Consider a parent who is telling her kids how lazy and mean-spirited her ex-husband is, or is arbitrarily denying him visitation because she knows how much he looks forward to the visits and this is her way of punishing him. In these instances, dads often feel their only recourse is to withhold or reduce support payments until their ex stops acting in this manner.

I would strongly urge every noncustodial parent to avoid withholding support payments. Such conduct can not only land you in jail, but it hurts your kids. In addition, every time you miss a payment in certain states, such as Illinois, a judgment is entered against you and interest accrues on the judgment, resulting in a hefty additional sum in a short period of time. Therefore, be forewarned. Even if you're not using nonpayment as a way to enforce your visitation—for example, if you lost your job and barely have enough money for food and rent, let alone anything else—don't assume that the court will be understanding. Your lawyer has to file an abatement or reduction of support petition, go to court, and win it.

If you're arguing with your ex-spouse about visitation and

custody issues, I would advocate following the suggestions previously described. As angry as your ex-spouse may make you, support is the wrong tool to use to exact justice. On the other hand, the following scenarios offer opportunities for both custodial and noncustodial parents to petition the court for a review and possible change of support provisions:

- Either parent experiences a significant change in income, such as through losing a job, receiving a pay increase, getting a new job that pays more than the old one, going back to work after being a stay-at-home parent, remarrying a spouse with significant income, or receiving a large inheritance.

- The custodial spouse moves with the kids to another area of the country where living expenses are significantly higher or lower and/or visitation-related expenses of the noncustodial parent increase.

- The noncustodial parent starts paying specific expenses directly (such as a child's educational costs or the mortgage on the custodial parent's home) that formerly were paid in part out of the support money.

- The custodial parent incurs unexpected large expenses related to the kids (such as uninsured medical costs).

Finally, you should be alert to the self-destructive or vengeful strategies that can cause you to lose your liberty and hurt your kids. A noncustodial spouse may go to all sorts of lengths to avoid paying money he can afford. His thought process may be twisted by anger at his ex-spouse, but that is no defense for hiding income or having an employer make under-the-table payments so that his support obligation is less than the amount the children need. Beware of rationalizing these actions. You may convince yourself that your ex is using some or most of the support money for her own purchases, such as new clothes, jewelry, or spa treatments. As a result, you feel good about your support scheme because you believe you're punishing your wife, not your kids, who aren't receiving the support money. If in fact your ex-spouse is guilty of these behaviors and your children are going hungry, wearing threadbare clothes, or having to discontinue dental care, then you need to gather evidence of her chicanery, go into court, and correct the problem.

Proving that an ex-spouse is misusing support money or hiding income often requires hiring a private detective. For instance, I represented a man whose wife owned a bar and claimed she needed a reduction in her support payment because business was off and she was making a very low sum of money annually. We hired a detective who sat in the bar for six hours a day for two weekends, wrote down how many people ordered drinks, and estimated the amount of money that came in during the six hour periods based on the number of drinks ordered. Shortly thereafter, we subpoenaed the books for those particular days and discovered that the amount of income my client's wife recorded in the books was far below the detective's estimate. The petition for reduced support was denied.

I'm not suggesting that people routinely defraud their ex-spouses and children of support money, or that custodial parents frequently use support money to buy luxuries for themselves and let their children go hungry or wear rags. In fact, suspicions of financial dishonesty may be nothing more than paranoia, and you would be well-advised to verify your suspicion with hard evidence before making an accusation in court. More than once, a client has come to me convinced that his wife was using his support money to buy jewelry that "must have cost her a grand at least," when it turned out that she'd bought a piece of costume jewelry for $25.

When custodial parents engage in schemes to defraud their ex-spouses involving support money, though, they usually have a more sophisticated plan than just buying things for themselves. Consider this scenario. Joan and Mark were married for nine years and have one child. The divorce stipulated a support amount that reflected Mark's excellent income and mandated that he maintain the payments until their child reach the age of majority, which was fifteen away. Shortly after the divorce became final, however, Joan asked Mark to give her a lump sum payment of all the money that he would be required to pay for the next fifteen years. She said that if he would do so, she would give him a thirty percent discount, so he would be paying considerably less money. Mark decided this was an excellent deal and agreed. Less than a year later, Joan disappeared with the lump sum payment, dropping the child off with her parents before leaving the country. Joan's parents were unaware of this lump sum arrangement, and they ended up suing Mark for support, which the court ordered him to provide. In essence, he was paying double support.

If your spouse suggests a lump sum payment in lieu of regular child support payments, that's fine as long as you go through an attorney and place the money in an irrevocable trust for the child with incremental payments to be made for him throughout his minority. The court should appoint an attorney for the child as well as approve the court-ordered lump sum payment. Remember, if your spouse uses the previous scheme, she may do so with malice aforethought. In other words, her initial impulse may be that she needs the money now to pay for significant expenses, but that over time she'll make more money and won't need to be dependent on you for future support. In reality, things may not work out as planned, or the lump sum payment may turn out to be too tempting to resist. In either case, if you're considering a lump sum payment, use the legal system and do so correctly.

POST-DECREE CRAZINESS

In some instances, mediation serves a dual purpose when post-decree disputes arise. Not only does it help parents deal with difficult custody, visitation, and financial issues, but it serves as a tool to help them adjust to being parents post-divorce. The anger, jealousy, and other negative emotions that often arise because one parent perceives the other to be better off needs to be dealt with, and a skilled mediator—especially one who is a good therapist—can help both people deal with these destructive emotions.

At least in some cases. In others, people become even more hostile toward their ex-mate than when they were married. For instance, Harold sought orders of protection against his ex-wife, Nina, in the initial years following their divorce. Even though she was engaged to another man and had never done anything even remotely threatening, Harold continued to ask for orders of protection. The reason: The mandatory court appearance meant he had a chance to see and sometimes briefly talk to Nina. In Harold's mind, all it would take was for Nina to see him in person and she would realize they belonged together. Needless to say, this didn't happen.

I've also seen ex-spouses argue about specific possessions long after the divorce was final. They may fixate on a particular object that wasn't specifically covered in the divorce agreement or that they feel was improperly given to the other party, and they demand to have it returned. When it isn't, they have their lawyer initiate legal proceedings to recover it, and the litigation sometimes costs far more than the object is worth. Objects range from works of art to heirlooms to photographs. I represented a womam who was married to her husband for seventeen years, and their post-decree dispute was over a pair of rose-colored candlesticks. You would have thought they were arguing over their kids, but instead they reserved their vitriol for the candlesticks and who should possess them. I found it telling that never once in those seventeen years had they ever lit the candles in them.

At the start of this chapter, I wrote that divorce is never really over, and I meant that it's not over even when child support, visitation, custody, and other issues no longer exist. I have seen ex-spouses fighting twenty or thirty years after the divorce, filing all manner of lawsuits against each other in an effort to redress what each feels was a terrible wrong. As much as I advise clients to let go of their anger and not use the legal system to exact vengeance, some people are intent on "getting even, no matter how long it takes." You need to consider whether your ex-spouse might come after you twenty or thirty years after the fact. You have to determine whether he or she is the sort of person who believes there is no statute of limitations on emotional pain.

CHAPTER EIGHT

Special Cases

Divorce wars tend to follow relatively predictable paths. Battles over visitation and custody are common. If one spouse is money-crazed, vengeful, or abusive, she may set up scenarios in which certain types of fights can be expected. As you just learned, post-decree skirmishes tend to fall into specific areas. My advice on what to do is predicated on events falling within the broad boundaries I've described.

In some situations, however, people cross the line. They exhibit unusual or even criminal behavior that requires a modified approach. I'd like to devote this chapter to these special cases. Specifically, I want to make sure you know what to do if:

- Your spouse kidnaps your child.

- You are charged with sexually abusing your child or you suspect your spouse is guilty of this crime.

- Your spouse is psychotic, delusional, or seriously "off" in some other way.

- Your spouse becomes involved with someone whom you feel poses a danger to your child.

- You and your spouse have a child but have never married.

- You and your spouse have reversed traditional roles—he is the stay-at-home parent and she is the one who works.

Though I've touched on some of these subjects in past chapters, I want to look at them in greater depth here. Some of them raise complex issues about which there is a great deal of misunderstanding—misunderstanding that might affect the outcome of your case. It also is wise to be prepared and prevent the first four items from affecting you or children negatively. Perhaps most important, though, each of these special cases illuminates how the divorce process really works. Unusual and extreme cases offer insights about our legal system and why divorce battles are won or lost. Even if your divorce war is more typical than the ones described here, I would bet that you'll learn something about orders of protection, remarriage, paternity, or dealing with enraged spouses that you can use in your divorce.

KIDNAPPING

You might think that a parent fleeing with a child is a rare occurrence, yet in fact, some estimates place the odds of it happening at one in every twenty-two divorce cases. When one parent is denied custody and his visitation privileges are limited, he may see no other option besides kidnapping his child. When children mean everything to a parent, then in his mind at least, risking jail may be preferable to being denied access to them. Similarly, some moms and dads don't even wait for a custody decision before they take off with their children. Convinced that the divorce process is going badly for them (or anticipating that it will go badly), they may become paranoid about the outcome and flee with the kids. For some, the stress and rage of a divorce combine to cause them to act irrationally; their twisted logic makes them feel that their spouse has done them an unforgivable harm, and that it is "fair" for them to strike back by taking the child.

I'd like to share two examples of child abduction to demonstrate how it can take place for very different reasons in very different ways. The first example involves a client of our firm, a man in the midst of a divorce who told us that he suspected his wife intended to take the kids and move to another state where she had relatives. We immediately obtained a court order that restrained and enjoined her from leaving. When the process server arrived at her residence, he found the mom and the kids loading up their van getting ready to move. He served her with the order, which she ignored, leaving that day for another state. We tracked her down and filed for contempt, and within a week the mom's lawyer contacted us and agreed to return the children to Illinois. Eventually we worked out a joint custody arrangement, and the mom and the kids remained in Illinois.

This story illustrates two points about parental kidnapping. First, be aware of how irrational people act when under the pressure of the divorce process. This mom ignored a court order, something few people in their right mind would do. No doubt it hurt her chances of getting sole custody and also put her liberty at risk. Just as significant, her insanity was temporary. Some people panic and run away with the kids, only to come to their senses after a bit of time has passed (and in this instance, a reality-inducing contempt order had been issued).

Now let me share a story about a recent case we handled, one referred to our firm by the National Center for Missing and Exploited Children. A man going through a divorce in Poland was on a trip in France when his Polish wife took their young son and came to Chicago to live. The man had no idea where she had gone, and we helped track her down. Once we found her, we filed suit in Chicago under the Hague Convention (an international treaty to which both the United States and Poland are signatories). Under this treaty, a U.S. judge could order the boy returned to Poland, and a Polish court could decide custody issues. Once we filed and my client's wife hired an attorney, we eventually reached a settlement in which the woman would continue to live in Chicago but the boy would return to Poland and see his dad for a month every summer and a week every Christmas, as well as at certain other times.

This case, too, raises a number of cautions about parental kidnapping. Most obviously, if you or your spouse (or both of you) is from a foreign country and you're going through a divorce, the possibility exists that she may flee with the children to or from that country. If both countries involved are signatories to the Hague Convention, then you have a tool to bring your spouse and kids back to your home country. Be aware, however, that this is easier said than done. The main obstacle is first finding your spouse and kids in another country, and you may need to hire a private investigator to do so. It's also important to understand that if one of the countries involved is not a signatory, then you're out of luck if you expect legal recourse under the Hague. I represented a woman whose spouse was from a paternalistic culture in the Middle East; her husband returned to his country with the children believing that the legal system there would be unsympathetic to his wife's wish for their return. Through creative and strategic planning, we helped the children to be returned to their mother in this country. Unfortunately, many children are not returned in these situations.

Kidnapping can be a well-planned, calculated act designed to separate one parent from his or her kids forever. This is true not only in international cases but in all types of divorces. I have seen both moms and dads create elaborate plans for covering their tracks and disappearing from sight. Therefore, it is absolutely essential for you to be alert to the signs that your spouse is considering abducting your kids.

Specifically, watch out for these behaviors:

- **Repeated threats to kidnap the child.** You would think this would send most people to their lawyers demanding emergency orders of protection against the parent making the threats, but many times people dismiss these threats as melodramatic emoting. Don't make this mistake, especially if the threat is made more than once. If you believe that your spouse is capable of carrying out the threats, you need to talk to your lawyer.

- **An unusual vacation or trip being planned.** By unusual, I mean that you notice something is different from your spouse's typical trip-taking modus operandi. Perhaps she is planning to visit a relative out of state whom she never visited before and claims to dislike. Maybe you find one-way tickets for herself and the kids hidden in the house. Or maybe you see your spouse packing her suitcase and her kids' bags for what she claims is a weekend trip, yet she's packing enough for at least a month-long stay.

- **Repeated phone calls to a friend or relative who lives outside your area.** These calls may mean nothing, but they also could be signs that plans are being made for flight.

- **Bringing passports on a trip that is supposedly to a place in this country.** This is an especially significant sign if your spouse is from a foreign country or has close friends or relatives there.

- **Your spouse is clearly upset by the direction the divorce is taking or by the judgment.** As I noted earlier, people who are strongly attached to their children and believe the divorce will end or diminish the relationship may be sufficiently upset to kidnap them. If this describes your spouse and he is also exhibiting one or more of the previously listed behaviors, he is a good candidate for being a child abductor.

I don't want to be an alarmist. Your spouse may tell you she and the children are going to visit her sister in another state, and her intent may be perfectly innocent. Before calling the police and accusing your wife of child abduction, talk over the situation with your lawyer. If he's experienced with these types of situations, he may be able to give you a good read on what's taking place. He may also suggest hiring a private detective to investigate if your spouse appears to be making plans to kidnap the children.

You can also take certain precautions that might deter your spouse from following through on a kidnapping impulse, or at least help you find him and the kids if she does commit this crime. Specifically, do the following if you suspect kidnapping is a possibility:

1. Do everything possible to create a fair custody and visitation agreement. I have found that it's rare for either a mom or a dad to abduct the children if a joint custody agreement is in place. Even if you receive sole custody, you can be generous with visitation. It's possible that your spouse is angry and abusive now and that the custody and visitation provisions reflect his emotional problems, but if you are willing to be flexible and amend the agreement when he gets control of himself, then he is much less likely to do something desperate.

2. Make it clear to your spouse that your expect her to be a consistent presence in your kids' lives, and this will go a long way to decreasing the odds of kidnapping.

3. Make sure the people who supervise your children (teachers, babysitters, child-care employees, bus drivers, coaches) are aware of the custody/visitation terms. Alert them if your spouse has made abduction threats. Instruct them not to release your kids to your spouse or anyone else if prohibited by court order. Ask to be notified immediately if the kids don't show up at any scheduled time and place.

4. Keep and continuously update a file containing "locating" information about your spouse and his close friends and relatives—phone numbers, addresses, license plate numbers, e-mail addresses, and so on.

5. Keep information about your children and your divorce handy—photos of the kids, copies of your custody and visitation orders—available at a moment's notice. Speed is often critical for recovery efforts if the kids are taken.

If your spouse makes a real threat to kidnap your children—if you possess strong evidence that your spouse is serious and the abduction is imminent—contact law enforcement officials. If they, too, take the threat seriously, they will inform your spouse that child abduction is a crime and explain the maximum sentence for committing this crime, which is severe. Your lawyer may also be able to obtain an emergency injunction or order of protection against your spouse prohibiting removal of your children from the state; he may also be able to obtain an order directing your spouse to turn over both her and her children's passports immediately to the court. All of these actions may deter a kidnapping, but you and your lawyer need to weigh the pros and cons of this action. Remember, the last thing you want to do is turn a skirmish into an all-out war. Don't let yourself become paranoid and turn an innocent remark into one that suggests your spouse intends to abduct your child.

If the worst happens—if you realize that your spouse has kidnapped your children—you must act immediately and follow the guidelines set forth by the National Center for Missing and Exploited Children. Here is a condensed version of some of their recommendations on www.ncmec.org:

- File a missing person's report with your local police department.

- Ask local authorities to have the FBI enter your children's description in their National Crime Information Center computer system.

- Call the NCMEC toll-free hot line at 1-800-843-5678 to report the children missing.

- Participate in the search for your kids; the NCMEC can assist by referring you to specific agencies and individuals.

- Meet with your local prosecutor and decide whether to press criminal charges. If your spouse has fled the state and is charged with a felony, the FBI may be able to assist in the search.

- If you don't have primary custody, obtain a temporary custody order with language directing the police and other government agencies to cooperate in the enforcement of this order. If you are the custodial parent, get certified copies of the custody decree from the court clerk. When your kids are found, send the copy to the family court in the jurisdiction where they were recovered.

- When the abductor is apprehended, ask the police to place the children in the court's care via a "pickup" order. Contrary to what you might think, the police usually aren't required to return your kids to you. You may need to petition the family court where your children are located to enforce your custody rights. The pickup order and participation of the police will help prevent your spouse from fleeing with the children when he is notified about the enforcement action if he is not incarcerated.

PHYSICAL AND SEXUAL ABUSE CHARGES

You'll note the word "charges" in the heading. If actual physical or sexual abuse has taken place—if your spouse has hurt your child or you in any way—then you must immediately inform your lawyer as well as the police to prevent any further abuse. If there are witnesses to the abuse or you have other clear proof that your spouse committed it, you can probably obtain an order of protection and either prevent the abusive parent from visiting the child or permit only strictly supervised visitation. Any parent who commits physical or sexual abuse during the divorce process will likely end up losing custody and unrestricted visitation privileges for a long time. If your spouse is beating you or your children or sexually abusing your kids, don't rationalize this behavior or tell yourself it's really not sexual abuse because it's only "innocent touching." Use the legal process to protect yourself and your children immediately as well as to get a psychological evaluation and treatment for your spouse.

With that said, however, I must admit that it is much more common during divorce wars for charges of abuse to be filed as part of legal strategy rather than because actual abuse was committed. One of the worst trends in family law in recent years is spouses feeling justified in filing false abuse charges. They tell themselves that their spouses have legal advantages because they are the breadwinners and possess superior financial resources— they can hire better attorneys, create a more convincing case by hiring expert witnesses, and exert financial pressure on the other party to settle. Whether or not these beliefs are true, they are often used as rationalizations for false abuse charges. The reasoning goes that these charges level the playing field, and the accusers intend to drop the charges as soon as their spouse agrees to a fair settlement.

While men make these false charges, women are more likely to be guilty of this particular dirty trick. As I've pointed out throughout this book, both men and women engaged in divorce wars exhibit all sorts of inflammatory and at times unethical behavior in order to win their case or punish their spouse. False charges of sexual abuse of kids, however, has become an increasingly common tactic for women involved in highly contentious divorces. Sometimes women suspect some type of sexual abuse took place—perhaps their child said something that made them think there was a problem—and not wanting to take a chance, they file charges. More often, however, they see an opportunity to use these charges to their advantage.

Traditionally, the courts bend over backwards to protect the rights of children, and even a faint hint that sexual abuse has been committed can be enough for the court to issue an order of protection against a dad and eliminate visitation or allow only supervised visitation. Women know that not only is it relatively easy to obtain these orders if they file charges, but it can take weeks or even months before the matter is resolved. During this time, the child doesn't see his father or sees him only under difficult circumstances. At times, this gives the mother a chance to alienate the child from his father. In addition, even if the charges are proven to be false, some judges may be unwilling to grant joint custody or unsupervised visitation to the father because they believe the child is scared of him—this is true even if the child has been brainwashed by the mom into believing the charges are accurate. Many times, years of therapy can be necessary to deprogram the child.

You should also understand that even when the charges are completely false, it is not that difficult for your spouse to present a credible case to a judge. She may be able to coach your child to say things that suggest abuse. Be aware that approximately 90 percent of sexual abuse charges during divorce cases involve children between the ages of three and five. They are usually too young to offer credible testimony, and they can be easily swayed by what they are told. In addition, a certain percentage of therapists are easily duped by mothers claiming sexual abuse. Some of these therapists have seen real cases of sexual abuse and are so outraged and horrified by these experiences that they sometimes see abuse when it doesn't exist. Other therapists simply don't understand to what lengths people are willing to go during a divorce war, and they don't believe any mother would ever make false sexual abuse charges against her husband.

If you're the victim of false sexual abuse charges, *do not* make the following three mistakes:

1. **Run to the police to protest your innocence and demand that they give you a lie detector test.** I have seen innocent men with the best of intentions go to the police on their own and end up saying things that are used against them in divorce court. They may deny ever sexually abusing their children, but admit that on occasion they hit them when they misbehave or confess to having been out of control when they were younger but that they have since shaped up. Inadvertently, they may say something that works against them in terms of custody or visitation. Therefore consult with your lawyer before you run to the police, and if you insist on visiting the authorities, bring your attorney with you.

2. **Give in immediately to any demand your spouse makes in order to get her to drop the abuse charges.** When men are falsely charged with sexually abusing a child they love, they are naturally upset and fearful. The fear often results in their caving in to whatever demands are being made. As difficult as it may be to allow those charges to stand one second more than they have to, it may be in your best interest to disprove them. Sometimes, just communicating to your spouse that you're going to fight the charges can cause her to drop them—litigating such charges can be expensive and time-consuming. You may also be able to prove that your spouse knowingly filed false sexual abuse charges—perhaps she told a friend or colleague of her plan—and if you can prove this, it can result in her losing custody. Therefore, talk with your lawyer about your other options before giving in.

3. **Become verbally abusive to either your spouse or investigators.** Typically, courts appoint a psychological evaluator to determine the validity of charges against you, the results of which are then passed on to the court. The evaluation process varies state by state, but you can expect to be interviewed (your child, spouse, and any other relevant parties will also be interviewed) and you will likely be observed interacting with your child during a play session. Your demeanor should be calm and cooperative. If you're hostile, sullen, or threatening, you will be seen as a potential abuser—you fit the profile. Therefore, keep your cool despite tough questions from the investigator.

How much do you have to worry if your spouse files sexual abuse charges against you? Generally, the evaluation process is fair and does a good job of clearing the innocent. If the evaluator is qualified, the process is gender-neutral, and you have skilled counsel, it should turn out okay. Investigators and judges are also well aware not only of the profile of sexually abusive parents, but of parents who file false charges. The following checklist contains specific behaviors and situations suggesting that abuse charges are fabricated. Place a check next to each item that applies to the charges against you:

- ❑ No sexual abuse charges have ever been filed against you prior to this one, either by the person divorcing you or in any previous relationships.
- ❑ Interrogatories, your spouse's deposition, and other discovery undertaken before these charges were filed contain no allegations of abuse.
- ❑ The divorce is highly combative, and fierce arguments are taking place regarding custody and visitation (and/or division of marital property, child support payments, and maintenance).
- ❑ You have recently become involved with another woman, and your wife is aware of this relationship.
- ❑ Your wife is verbally abusive toward you, vengeful, and greedy; she has harped on the need to put you in jail, even before the evaluation has started.
- ❑ Your spouse has suggested that she might drop the charges in exchange for the house, a larger support or maintenance payment, or some other financial benefit.
- ❑ Your spouse acts irrationally and has a history of mental illness or psychological problems.
- ❑ If your child has verified your wife's charges, the child's account is very similar to the mother's report in terms of phrasing and narrative structure.

❏ Your child's responses about the abuse appear to be rehearsed or coached; she uses descriptions not appropriate for her age and doesn't seem to understand what she is saying.
❏ Your child isn't nervous or uncomfortable in your presence.
❏ Your child is between the ages of three and five.

Even if you have numerous check marks, that doesn't mean that an investigator or judge will immediately conclude that you're innocent of the sexual abuse charges. They may, however, place a much greater burden of proof on the accuser.

Finally, though I've defended many fathers against false sexual abuse charges of children, false charges of physical abuse are not unheard of. Both men and women have been known to hurt themselves and claim that their spouse beat them. They are so furious at their husband or wife for filing divorce papers that they want charges of battery filed against that person. In most instances, these false charges are difficult to prove—it's one person's word against the other's—and if you have no history of physical abuse of your spouse or children and no prior battery convictions, it's unlikely that the charges will stick. It's also possible that as your spouse's anger subsides, the false charges will be dropped.

A DANGEROUS NEW PERSON IN YOUR CHILD'S LIFE

As the divorce process unfolds, one of the most difficult things for you to deal with will be the new person in your spouse's life. Whether he remarries or simply has a live-in girlfriend, the situation may cause you to be jealous, angry, or sad. Legally, it's a nonissue under most circumstances, but individual state laws vary here. Even if you feel he's involved with a gold digger, it's seldom going to affect the divorce. Even if he has moved in with your former best friend and you're certain he did so vengefully, you have no legal recourse in most instances. If, however, he is spending marital assets on this girlfriend, then he may have caused dissipation of the marital estate, for which he could be held accountable. In some states, you can sue the new person in your spouse's life for "alienation of affections," but financial recovery is limited to actual damages.

However, you should contemplate aggressive and speedy legal action if the new person in your spouse's life poses a threat to your child or actually harms him physically or emotionally in some way. In these instances, your attorney can file for an order of protection, removal of your child from the household in which he is endangered, sole custody, or supervised visitation. The tricky issue, however, is what constitutes "harm." There is fuzzy legal line separating physical abuse from disciplinary actions. If, for instance, your spouse's boyfriend swatted your child on the rear end once when he misbehaved, it's unlikely that this single incident would be grounds for any of the legal actions previously noted. On the other hand, if this boyfriend breaks your child's leg or shows a pattern of imposing injurious physical discipline, this probably is grounds for removal and an order of protection, assuming you have strong evidence of the abuse. This can also result in the boyfriend being criminally charged with battery or more.

The following is a list of reasons that may constitute a cause for legal action:

- Corporal punishment that causes bruising, bleeding, or burning.

- Denial of food, water, shelter, or medical treatment.

- Derogatory language or conduct designed to destroy a child's self-esteem.

- Berating or humiliating a child frequently in the presence of friends, family, teachers, or others.

- Any type of sexual abuse.

- Exposing the child to bad influences, including an environment where someone is continually using alcohol or drugs.

People often assume that if they remarry or move in with someone, it will not have any impact on custody or visitation as long as no direct physical or emotional abuse of the child occurs. This is not always a correct assumption. If the courts find that the parent's new relationship is likely to affect the child in negative ways, there does not have to be direct abuse of the child.

For example, I represented Bill, who was the father of Jenny, an eight-year-old girl. Bill had filed for divorce from his wife, Nancy, when he discovered that she was having an affair with Lucy, who was eighteen. During the divorce, Lucy moved in with Nancy, and at that point Bill petitioned the court for sole custody. What disturbed Bill was that Nancy, who was a nurse at a chemical rehabilitation center, had become involved with Lucy when she was a patient at the center. Not only did he find his wife's behavior unethical, but the more he learned about Lucy the more he wanted to keep Jenny away from her. He discovered that Lucy had been a drug abuser and had been "clean" for only a short period of time. Even more troubling, she had written Nancy letters that revealed she had been sexually abused as a child and that she had violent dreams, including one in which she killed Jenny.

The court awarded Bill sole custody, not because Lucy had ever done or said anything that harmed Jenny, but because of a combination of factors—her drug use, her emotional instability, and Nancy's misuse of her position of authority to start an affair with her.

I should emphasize that just because your spouse reveals he or she is gay and takes a same-sex lover, that alone does not affect how the court views the gay parent's child-raising ability or the environment in which the child is being raised. It is only when other factors enter the picture—emotional instability of the new person in your child's life, for instance—that the court will consider that person a negative influence.

CHILDREN OUT OF WEDLOCK

Approximately 33 percent of children in this country are born out of wedlock. In Chicago and other large cities, the statistic is often over 50 percent. Beyond the terrible social problems these statistics suggest, they also create problems for couples who break up. Consider these scenarios.

Two people have been living together for a number of years, and the woman becomes pregnant. The man gets scared and doesn't feel that he can be responsible for a child, so he leaves. Does this man have any rights as the father of the child, even though he left of his own volition? What if he stays away for a year or two, and then decides he wants to know and support his child? What rights does the woman have if the man has shown no interest in the child for a significant period of time? How can she protect the child from the father's returning, establishing a relationship with the child, and then running away again?

Here's the second scenario. A couple has had a child and lived together for seven years, raising the child together. Then the woman meets another man, who wants to marry her and adopt their child. The woman tells the father to move out and that he can never see his child again. What rights does he have in this situation?

These are just two of many situations in which an informal breakup causes many of the same problems as a formal divorce. In most instances, fathers who register in a timely manner with the putative father registry (if applicable in your state) and establish legal paternity immediately, provide financial support for the child from pregnancy onward, and are consistently involved in their child's life will likely retain the same rights as any married parent and have the same obligations. They will be expected to pay support and probably will also receive visitation privileges, and even joint custody arrangements are possible.

The U.S. Supreme Court ruled in 1983 that the parental rights of unmarried fathers are "perishable." In other words, you have to "use it or lose it." If you desert your child early on and fail to provide any financial assistance from the time the child is born, you may find it difficult to assert your rights as a parent later, especially if you return after a long absence.

If you're an unwed father and want to maintain your parental rights, you should consider establishing paternity through a court order. This is not a substitute for acting like a dad—for providing emotional and financial support for your child—but it is relatively easy to do and provides legal recognition. In most states, all that is required is that you and the other parent sign an agreed order that needs to be subsequently entered by a judge. However, you should undergo a DNA test before signing this order to make sure you are the biological father. Paternity fraud and "father shopping" are two good reasons for DNA testing.

If you're an unwed mother and want to obtain child support

from the father, you must usually file a paternity suit, and the individual in question will probably undergo a DNA test to determine whether he's the father. If he is, he is liable for the same support payments as he would be if you had been married and divorced. It's important to point out that children born out of wedlock may enjoy the same rights to child support as children of married parents.

Finally, if you never married, your child may be adopted by another individual, usually the person whom the other parent of the child marries. In terms of this adoption process, many states have laws declaring that a "good faith" effort should be made to locate and inform the biological parent of the adoption. In reality, this doesn't always occur. Therefore, the adoption may take place without your knowledge. If you're aware of it, you can attempt to contest the adoption. This means, at the very least, filing a defense to the adoption stating that you will not consent to it. Be aware that your chances of successfully contesting the adoption often depend on acting as quickly as possible. If it can be proved that you knew about the baby and did nothing for years, then it may be difficult to prevent the adoption. If, on the other hand, you can prove that as soon as you realized you had a child you made a concerted effort to visit him, you have a much better chance to assert your parental rights in an adoption case. In such a case, you should search long and hard for a sharp lawyer who understands the legal intricacies of contesting an adoption.

SWITCHING TRADITIONAL GENDER ROLES

Some people find themselves in pitched battles during their divorce because they switched gender roles: The man stayed at home and took care of the kids while the mom was the breadwinner. When they decided to get divorced, however, the woman believed her gender entitled her to custody while the man was certain his stay-at-home role meant he should receive custody.

If you find yourself in this position, you should know that if you're a man, you have a better chance of gaining custody and if you're a working woman, you have a better chance of losing it or accepting a joint custody agreement. At the same time, much depends on your jurisdiction and judge. In some parts of the country, judges still favor traditional custody arrangements in which women are the primary caregivers. Other judges, however, recognize that if a man has been the primary caregiver for a sustained period of time and sacrificed a career to be that caregiver, then consideration should be given to the relationship that the man has forged with his kids.

Nonetheless, I've seen some of the most acrimonious divorce battles occur between spouses who switched roles. Gary, for instance, quit a high-paying job as a corporate attorney to help raise all three of his children. Gary's wife, Marge, was an advertising executive who continued to work long hours and travel extensively after the children were born. When their three kids were 11, 8, and 5, Gary had an affair with a neighbor. Marge found out about it and initiated divorce proceedings. Marge was adamant that she receive custody, in large part because she knew how much the kids meant to Gary and how her insistence on sole custody would torture him. Gary was just as stubborn about not allowing Marge to have custody, making the argument that she frequently missed parent-teacher conferences at school, was out of town at least one week each month, and routinely worked sixty-hour weeks; he said that if Marge received custody, she would simply hire someone to parent the children for her. Neither Gary nor Marge would given an inch. In initial settlement conferences, they would engage in terrible screaming matches and once had to be restrained from physical combat. When negotiations broke down, the case went to trial, and it was only through the efforts of a savvy judge that the couple grudgingly compromised and reached a last-minute settlement before he handed down a judgment. They settled on joint custody with a number of provisos, including that Marge would not hire a nanny or other child-care provider when she had the kids and that Gary would have to return to the workforce to contribute to their support (Marge said that because of joint custody, she could not work the hours her boss expected and would probably not receive another promotion at any point in the near future).

The point of this story is that if you have switched roles, it is unlikely that you'll be able to maintain your current lifestyle and work style after the divorce. To avoid the stressful, time-consuming, and expensive divorce that Gary and Marge endured, it is better to reach a compromise sooner rather than later. If you're the stay-at-home dad, you're probably going to have to return to the workforce. If you're the working mom, you may have to reduce the hours you spend at the office or find a new, less demanding job. Without these compromises, you may end up in an internecine war that can only be settled by a judge.

YOU'RE DEALING WITH A CRAZY PERSON

I've saved the worst for last. As I've alluded to in earlier chapters, some spouses become crazed when they find their husbands or wives have filed for divorce and some become increasingly irrational as the process unfolds. I have been involved in cases where one spouse has become so unhinged that he has threatened or even committed murder. I have seen other people become depressed and suicidal. More commonly, however, people's craziness during the divorce manifests itself as a desire to hurt their spouse financially and emotionally. The divorce becomes a tool to inflict pain on their mate, and they are willing to sacrifice time, money, and even their children to inflict this pain.

Here, I'm not just referring to someone who acts irrationally for a few days or weeks and then snaps out of it, or someone who is going through the divorce bitter and angry but still acts rationally. I've listed this as a special situation for a reason. It's not common for a spouse to fight to the death over a pair of candlesticks, as I mentioned in the previous chapter. Nor is it typical for someone to be willing to spend every penny he possesses in order to drag out the divorce process and his wife's emotional suffering as long as he can. Thankfully, the majority of cases don't involve these types of people, but if your spouse is one of them, you can do some things to protect yourself and your kids from the craziness. Obviously, if the irrational behavior puts you or your children in physical danger, you can usually obtain an order of protection and limit visitation. To deal with a less urgent situation, here are some strategies that, however, here are some strategies that I've found sometimes helps a crazy acting spouse calm down a bit during the divorce:

- **Have your attorney suggest to your spouse's attorney that his client might need to see a psychiatrist.** If you tell your spouse he should see a shrink, he'll probably resist the suggestion and become even more irrational than he already is. If the suggestion comes from his lawyer, on the other hand, he might take it more seriously. No attorney wants to have a crazy person as a client—at least no ethical attorney does. People who aren't acting rationally are likely to do or say things that will hurt the outcome of their case. Therefore, the attorney may be able to couch the suggestion in a way that his client finds palatable. While psychiatrists can't work miracles, and there's only a limited amount of time for the divorce process to unfold, they may be able to provide medication that will make your spouse more rational or at least give him a place to vent his anger at someone besides you.

- **Make concessions you can live with.** I've seen more than one irrational, raging client calm down when his spouse made a few concessions. This is especially true when the irrational spouse is paranoid and believes that she is getting nothing while her husband is getting everything. As soon as he says, "Okay, you can have the car" or "I'll give you the big-screen television," it takes the edge off her crazy behavior. I'm not saying you should give up something that you deeply care about or give your spouse unlimited visitation if you feel that would be bad for your kids. I'm just suggesting that what you lose by your concessions, you gain by restoring some semblance of rational behavior to your spouse.

- **Make the best-interest-of-the children argument.** When it comes to you, your spouse may act crazy. But when his focus is on the children, he probably acts in a more logical, clear-headed manner. Instead of arguing about who should get the house, turn the argument into how the children will be affected if you must sell the house. Instead of getting stuck on the number of hours per week he'll be allowed to visit, examine what activities are especially important for him to do with the kids. By redirecting the argument in this manner, your spouse may actually listen for a moment instead of being consumed by his own obsessions.

- **Don't allow your spouse to see that her behavior is getting to you.** When your crazed spouse sees that something she said or did got to you, she is like a shark swimming with blood in the water. She is so consumed by her own demons that all she wants is to make you as miserable as she is. When she is able to do so, she is empowered to do more of the same. Therefore, do everything possible to remain in emotional neutral. During negotiations, refrain from making sarcastic comments, crying, or engaging in screaming matches. Don't tell mutual friends how upset she is making you, since it will surely get back to her. If you must go to court, maintain a stoic demeanor whether you're on the stand or just observing.

Admittedly, people who are acting in strange or manic ways are the most difficult to deal with during a divorce. Sometimes, you can't do anything but sit there and take it, comforting yourself with the knowledge that you had the sense to divorce this person before the behavior became even worse. If you're lucky, though, your spouse has not gone completely around the bend, and one or more of these four strategies will calm him down enough to make the divorce less costly, time-consuming or stressful than it might otherwise become.

CHAPTER NINE

Future Wars, Current Realities: What We Must Do to Manage the Battles

There are no statistics that measure the degree of acrimony in divorce cases. From a purely empirical standpoint, however, any divorce lawyer worth his salt will tell you that the battles are more frequent and more fierce now than at any time in the past. This is due in part to the nature of our society. Some men's and women's groups have escalated the rhetoric, the former convincing men that if they don't fight, they'll lose their kids figuratively and literally to heartless women; the latter convincing women that if they don't fight for their rights, they will be taken advantage of by heartless men. While both these fears may be well-founded in certain situations, in many others they are baseless.

The media, too, reinforces stereotypical notions about gender and divorce. From television shows to movies to commercials, the media delights in stories that turn every divorce into a tale of good versus evil. When ordinary people get divorced, these fictional stories make everyone suspect the worst: that their spouse is plotting to steal their kids, their money, and their property. Obviously from the stories in this book, you're aware that these types of things do take place. Unfortunately, these warlike divorces are often the result of a self-fulfilling prophecy. People refuse to settle because they are convinced the settlement offer is a ploy. Rather than examine the reality of a situation, using the analytical approach recommended in these pages, they are operating purely on emotion. If they're furious with their spouse, they automatically assume the worst and figure he'll behave exactly the way some cad did on their favorite soap opera.

Finally, our culture of victimhood is making a bad situation worse. People don't take accountability for their actions. If they have an affair and it ruins the marriage, they don't accept the blame. Instead, they look at their spouse and say, "She made me do it." During a divorce, this translates into people digging in and refusing to accept responsibility for the dissolution of the marriage. They refuse to provide a reasonable amount of child support, split the assets fairly, or allow visitation that will help the noncustodial parent maintain a good relationship with the kids. Why? Because "I gave in to him on everything from A to Z during our marriage and I'm not going to give in now. He's the reason we're getting divorced." When people feel like victims, they become intractable and refuse to give an inch. Thus, divorce wars.

In this last chapter, I want to give you a sense of the trends that will affect these wars now and in the future. I don't see any of the just-noted factors disappearing, but I do see both good and bad trends emerging that may change both the battles and battlegrounds of divorce. More important, I have found that there are ways of responding to these trends that can make divorce a manageable process rather than all-out war, and I'll share these ideas with you as well.

ALIMONY ALL OVER AGAIN

Many years ago, in the era of stay-at-home moms and working dads, alimony was common. The presumption was that a wife's nonpaying job was to take care of the children, prepare meals, and otherwise support her husband's efforts to make a living for the family. During a divorce, therefore, alimony was an acknowledgment of a wife's contributions and her right to share in the financial bounty her work at home made possible. With the dawning of the feminist era, equal rights, and women rejoining the workforce in droves, alimony became an anachronism. In fact, until the early 1990s, nonworking custodial parents received very little besides a division of the marital assets and child support; they were expected by the courts to rejoin the workforce and make their own way.

In the early 1990s, however, we saw a shift in many jurisdictions, and courts began handing out maintenance freely. In part, this was a backlash against the movement that encouraged women to do it all and go back to work three months after having a baby. Many judges, especially older ones, believed that having moms stay at home with the kids at least through early childhood was good for the kids. Therefore, they awarded them maintenance routinely, even when they possessed substantial marital assets.

Increasingly, we're seeing fights revolving around maintenance, whether there are kids or not. This is due in part to the differing interpretations of who deserves maintenance and how much it should be. We represented one man, an executive making a good but not great salary. He was married to a woman who previously was a well-paid lawyer but had quit her job a few years before the divorce filing to open a small antiques store. There were no children and this should have been a relatively simple divorce, but it turned into a major battle that eventually went to trial. This man was furious that his wife was demanding maintenance. While it was true her antiques shop was making little money, he felt that she was perfectly capable of obtaining a well-paying job with a law firm any time she wanted, and he accused her of asking for maintenance from him as vengeance. She in turn said that she had been the major earner early in their marriage when he went back to school to obtain his MBA, that the antiques store was her dream, and that she had used her own money earned years ago as a lawyer to open it. She accused her husband of hating that she was doing something that made her happy and that he was well aware that she'd been extremely unhappy as a lawyer. Eventually, the court awarded her a modest amount of maintenance that made neither our client nor his ex-spouse particularly happy. The confusion over maintenance, though, had fanned the flames and made it impossible for the couple to reach a settlement.

What is adding to the confusion is the concept of "standard of living of the marriage." More and more, we're seeing judges use this standard as a justification for maintenance awards. In one case in which we were involved, John, an engineer who made a decent salary, was married to Marge, who had a clerical job. They also had two children, and John won custody of both of them. Marge, therefore, could easily live on the money she made from her job. The problem was that she could not live in the style to which she had become accustomed. The standard of living of the marriage was higher than she could afford on her own. Therefore, the judge ordered John to pay Marge sufficient maintenance so she could at least approach that standard.

As you can imagine, this concept makes many people's blood boil—both men and women. Increasingly, women are the major earners in some families, and they are outraged when a judge orders them to pay maintenance to their spouse, especially when their spouse was the one who filed for the divorce or left her for another, younger woman.

One positive trend on the maintenance front, however, is the growing acceptance of "rehabilitative maintenance" as an appropriate way to provide maintenance. Instead of a no-strings-attached cash payment, rehabilitative maintenance is like a scholarship. It's designed to help one spouse go back to school or obtain additional job training as well as support himself during this time so that he can get a better-paying job than would have been possible without the education or training. If rehabilitative maintenance becomes the new, commonly accepted standard, then it will likely diminish fights in this area.

I should make one additional side note that might surprise you. When it comes to maintenance awards, many women often want to have a female judge who they believe will identify with their plight. In the past, this may have made sense. Today, though, we're seeing an increasing number of female judges reluctant to provide women with sizable amounts of maintenance. My theory is that many younger female judges have worked very hard throughout their marriage and taken only a brief amount of time off when they had children. When a woman asks for maintenance, their thinking often is, "I worked through marriage and kids (and possibly their own divorce); why can't you?" Therefore, their ruling on maintenance may come with the expectation that a nonworking woman will rejoin the workforce or that someone who is working but not making much money will find a better-paying job.

MORE JOINT CUSTODY AWARDS

What gives me hope that the divorce process may become a bit kinder and gentler in the future is the trend toward more joint custody awards. Even in the mid-1980s, little support for joint custody existed. The rationale then was that divorcing parents couldn't get along during their marriage, so how could they work together and help raise their kids if one person didn't have sole decision-making power? The prospect of endless arguments that hurt rather than helped children pushed judges in the direction of sole custody. Over time, however, this attitude has changed. Both in the legal and therapeutic communities, evidence has mounted that joint custody is often a better option than sole custody. Therapists have concluded that kids need both their parents (unless one is abusive), and that to deny a child regular access to one parent can do irreparable harm. Similarly, as the legal community has tested joint custody in practice, they have found that more often than not, parents who feuded during a marriage put aside their differences afterwards in the best interest of the child. Once the divorce is final and most of the issues have been resolved, parents are often able to rise above their animosity and find ways to work with each other to make good decisions for their kids. In addition, many judges are aware that a joint custody award is a good way to prevent the battle between parents from raging long after the divorce is over. When one parent receives custody and the other doesn't, resentment naturally builds in the disenfranchised parent and a sense of entitlement arises in the custodial parent. This creates more tension and arguments, and kids are the ones who suffer.

Joint custody moderates these negative effects in most instances. Of course, if it's joint custody in name only, it will catalyze more post-divorce wars. Some of the new joint custody agreements I've read aren't worth the paper they're written on. The language of these agreements makes it clear that while both parents share custody in principle, one parent has it in fact. They dictate that the parent with whom the child lives will make all the decisions affecting that child. While the agreements usually include clauses that declare all decisions must be discussed jointly by both parents, they only create the illusion of shared decision-making.

Just as problematic, some agreements mandate joint decision-making but lack a mandatory dispute resolution clause. This is a critical omission, since there will be times when parents have honest disagreements that can flare into destructive battles without a resolution clause. Many times, I've seen disagreements occur around issues such as whether a child should go to public or private school, and each parent takes a position that he or she truly believes in. Without dispute resolution, the disagreement escalates—the dad accuses his ex-spouse of "wasting money on private school like you waste on everything else that's not important." The mom accuses her ex-spouse of "putting your checking account before your child." All of a sudden, a disagreement that might have been civil and contained becomes uncivil and spills into other areas. Effective alternative dispute resolution clauses are necessary in case of a disagreement, and they should name a specific person as a mediator to resolve the dispute and list a backup if the first selection isn't available. This enables the dispute to be dealt with quickly and by a competent professional. These are essential steps, since disputes that simmer for too long often boil over and end up in court.

Finally, joint custody agreements should also be reviewed regularly. Ideally, the agreements will be subject to annual reviews. In this way, parents don't have to "wing it" or go back to court when circumstances change. If, for instance, the parent with whom the child lives has to start traveling more for business, it may make sense to change the child's residence during that period of travel. I've found, too, that as children become older, many things may change. One parent who insisted that he always do certain activities with a child when that child was a toddler may become less controlling when the child is a preteen, willingly ceding certain parenting tasks to his ex-spouse. It may also be more important for a dad to spend more time with his son when he reaches adolescence and needs the discipline and role model that a same-sex parent provides. By reviewing these agreements annually, you can discuss changes, revise the agreement, and avoid what otherwise might become points of contention, resulting in litigation.

INCREASINGLY COMPLEX SITUATIONS

As a general rule, the more complex a divorce is, the more likely it is to turn into a war. When the marital assets are significant and varied, dividing them fairly can require wisdom beyond what most lawyers possess. We're seeing people who are divorcing after twenty or more years coming in with all manner of benefits plans—401(k), profit-sharing, traditional pensions, stock ownership, and so on. If both spouses have been working and have these plans, it becomes difficult to determine a fair division of assets. This is especially true if one parent stayed at home and helped raise the kids and returned to the workforce later, made less money, and had less to put in her plans. Similarly, we're now going through a period where people are inheriting more money than ever before, and the size of these inheritances coupled with the language of wills and how the inherited nonmarital money sometimes is transmuted (sometimes unknowingly) into marital property often complicates matters. As a result of all this, people argue when the time comes to split the assets. Sometimes, the impact the split will have on each person's future (such as affecting when someone will be able to retire) combined with the difficulty of sorting out who gets what causes emotional outbursts.

Even more problematic, however, is the growing complexity of family situations. Unlike years past, many men today start second families when they're in their forties or even older. For instance, they might start their first family when they're in their twenties, and then fifteen years later get divorced, meet and marry a younger woman, have a second group of kids, and get divorced again. In many states, the woman and children in the second divorce receive less money than the wife and kids in the first divorce, the fact being that there's often less money available for support the second time around. While this may be financially fair, try telling that to the second wife. Understandably, she feels like she's getting the short end of the stick. She argues for more money, he claims he can't afford it, and the argument escalates all the way to divorce court.

In addition, where there are multiple kids from multiple marriages, visitation situations can become a logistical nightmare. Fights over scheduling are more the rule than the exception, and inevitable conflicts arise that increase one parent's frustrations to the point that she may file a Motion for a Modification (a reduction) of Visitation.

Grandparents' rights, too, are an emerging issue that complicates matters. We live in society where grandparents often spend more time with small children than their parents do. When both mom and dad have to work, the grandparents are responsible for child care. In many instances, the retired grandparents may be with the child for forty hours or more every week. When the divorce happens, however, the situation may change. The parent who receives custody may no longer want or need her spouse's parents to continue to care for the child. In turn, the grandparents may file a Motion for Visitation, especially if they, along with their adult child, are cut out of their grandchild's life. The courts are acknowledging that grandparents do indeed have rights in these matters, especially if they have been an integral part of a child's life for a sustained period of time and a clear bond has been established. Of course, the divorcing parent who feels the grandparents have been a pain may not feel this bond is emotionally healthy and he may be glad to get rid of them. In fact, this parent may try to make the case that the grandparents have had a negative influence on the child—he may attempt to prove that they are religious fanatics, for instance. As a result, a variation on the typical divorce war ensues.

Finally, there's one more factor that can make divorce cases much more complex these days, though we haven't seen the factor as the cause of much litigation—yet. Donor dads—men who donate their sperm to women who aren't their spouses in order to have babies—are sure to catalyze legal fights in the future. At some point, we're bound to see more lawsuits filed when the donor dad wins the lottery or comes into a lot of money in some other way; the mother of his child may demand child support payments from this now-wealthy donor. Common sense may tell you that this is unlikely to happen, that a clear bargain was struck between the donor and the woman, and a legal document was written and signed that denied the donor all parental rights and relieved him of all obligations. Similarly, the open adoption trend is bound to create problems down the road. As more and more couples adopt children and allow their biological moms to be known to one and all, legal problems will result. What happens when the adopting parents decide to divorce—will the biological mom step in and request custody? What if the adopting couple doesn't divorce but the biological mom believes that they are raising her child in a harmful way? We've seen a lawsuit here and there regarding these issues, but I fully expect many more in the years to come.

If you're involved in one of these complex situations, I recommend finding an attorney who has extensive experience dealing with these complexities. As I mentioned earlier, some family lawyers are ill equipped to handle anything but a run-of-the-mill divorce. Some decent family lawyers may never have dealt with a multiple-family divorce or may not be up to speed on the legal issues involved in dividing myriad benefit-plan monies and other extensive marital assets. Therefore, be sure to ask your attorney about whether she has handled cases similar to the one in which you're involved, and don't be shy about requesting to talk to former clients.

PEARL HARBOR STRIKES

As the title of this section implies, some spouses launch sneaky, immoral attacks during a divorce; these people should expect the attacked party to fight back. Until relatively recently, we seldom saw orders of protection being used to punish a spouse and alienate him from his kids; today, these orders are being abused frequently. Typically, what happens is an emerging ex parte hearing is held at the start of the divorce, and one party asks the court for an order of protection against her spouse who was not present because he was not notified of the court date (notice is not required). This individual may go by herself and request the assistance of a domestic violence advocate or bring her attorney with her. In either case, if this order of protection is granted, she often receives temporary possession of the children and exclusive possession of the marital residence, as well as other relief. In addition, if the spouse against whom this order of possession was entered even inadvertently ends up in the same building as his spouse, he could face criminal charges for violating the order of protection and end up in jail.

If this individual is guilty of threatening or hurting either his spouse or kids, this order is justified. If, however, the order of protection is used as a tactic to negotiate favorable custody, visitation, or financial terms of the divorce, than it is just plain wrong and guaranteed to create animosity and legal battles for years to come. Imagine that you were wrongly accused of being a physical threat to your wife and kids. Think about how you would feel knowing that your kids were aware of this order and may well have been convinced by your spouse that you made the threats she fabricated. Even worse, imagine yourself standing on the front lawn stuffing your possessions into a trash bag with the police standing guard and your neighbors watching. If this were you, you likely would be ready to fight your spouse on every point possible for years to come.

The best way to curtail Pearl Harbor strikes is for the courts to impose financial sanctions on spouses and their attorneys when the basis for an order of protection charge proves groundless. I recognize that proving these orders were entered without merit would require even more legal actions and costs, but the simple existence of sanctions would discourage the filing of false petitions seeking these orders. Right now, nothing deters people from using these orders as a negotiation ploy, and sanctions would make this strategy risky, especially for lawyers.

POLITICIZING CHILD SUPPORT

This is a terrible trend, but it's one that has gained momentum in states throughout this country. No one wants to be viewed as supporting parents who shirk paying child support, and that fear seems to drive some politicians to turn child support into a political crusade. Everyone from sheriffs to legislators has sponsored actions that can only be described as punitive measures when dads can't pay. The names of deadbeat dads are published in local newspapers, their driver's licenses are suspended for failure to pay, or they are thrown in jail. No doubt, these measures are called for in a relatively small number of cases—there are men who have the money to pay but don't because they see nonpayment as vengeance against their spouse, or they just aren't very good people and parents. The majority of the time, however, dads who can't keep up with payments have lost jobs, are struggling with medical problems, or have other issues that prevent them from making payments. These are not deadbeat dads but dead broke dads.

Dads who are humiliated, jailed, or deprived of their driver's licenses will be even less likely to pay support in the future than they were in the past. If you are a cab driver unable to find a new job because you're prevented from driving, how in the world can you keep up with your payments? In addition, dads who are labeled and punished often tell themselves, "What's the use?" If they have made a good-faith effort to make their support payments but an event beyond their control has caused them to fall behind, the last thing that should happen is their humiliation and punishment. This is what makes some men lose their motivation to find jobs, become depressed, or even commit suicide.

It also contributes to the internecine battles in which the

children once again are victims. What typically happens is that dads fall behind on their support payments because of a lost job or an unexpected expense. Moms, caught up in the politicized, punitive atmosphere, tell them they don't care why they've fallen behind, they won't be allowed to see their kids until they come up with the money. Dads respond, "Well if I can't see the kids, I'm not giving you another penny."

The solution here is for the politicians and courts to distinguish between immoral deadbeat dads and good fathers who are making honest efforts to pay support but for one reason or another can't do it. As an incentive for this solution, let me add that studies show that the more parental involvement and visitation a dad has, the more likely he is to pay child support. Positive reinforcement, such as dads receiving encouragement to become more involved in their children's lives, will motivate men to find ways to meet their support obligations.

FOLLOWING IN MOM'S AND DAD'S FOOTSTEPS: THE NEW DIVORCE

People in their twenties and thirties have witnessed their parents' divorce wars. While older people may have had divorced parents, this tends to be the exception rather than the rule. Today, many young people are disillusioned by their experiences growing up in households where their parents fought constantly, not only while they were married but during and after their divorce. Some of these people have vowed never to get married, preferring to just date or live with another person. Eventually, though, many of them will warily decide they want to raise a family and get married, vowing not to repeat the mistakes of the past.

Unfortunately, these young people have had poor role models when it comes to both marriage and divorce. Invariably, some of them will fall into the same behavioral patterns that have been modeled for them. It is disturbing to see the degree of cynicism and pessimism many young people have when it comes to marriage. I fear that their doubts about the possibility of sustaining a marriage may become a self-fulfilling prophecy.

Even worse, as the lines between gender roles have blurred, they will have more issues to fight about. In the near future, we will see a rise in the number of stay-at-home dads, in the number of two-income households where moms make more money than dads, and in situations where high-earning moms feel guilty and decide to quit their jobs to stay at home with their kids. All this will be grist for the divorce mill. We're going to see more dads wanting sole custody and more women paying them child support and maintenance; it would not surprise me if the term "deadbeat mom" is coined.

All this is troubling, especially when you consider the children; they will be caught in the middle. The last thing you want to see are people reaching for the phone and calling divorce lawyers reflexively. In the past, divorce was generally a last resort and not undertaken lightly. In the future, it may be an option seized too quickly and too easily. Remember, the younger generation has been conditioned to divorce realities. They may see the shelf life of a marriage as being ten years or less. They may accept that they're going to get divorced and that they're going to have to fight it out to obtain a fair settlement.

I hope I'm wrong about this last trend. What might increase the odds that I'll be wrong is if certain reforms are made to the divorce process.

HOW TO MAKE THE PROCESS BETTER . . .
FOR BOTH THE PARENTS AND THE KIDS

I'm not naïve. I know that change to any area of the law comes slowly and that many parties have a vested interest in maintaining the status quo. Nonetheless, I'm optimistic that incremental improvements can be made and over time the system can become more responsive to the needs of parents and children. In my efforts on behalf of father's rights over the years, I've seen positive changes occur that have helped dads in many ways. I remember co-authoring the joint custody law in Illinois years ago when many of my colleagues felt such a law wasn't possible. The system still isn't perfect, but it's better than it was before.

I hope the same type of changes can make divorce a less stressful, costly, and divisive process for everyone involved. Throughout this chapter and throughout the book, I've emphasized how you can deal with the system that is currently in place to moderate the stress and costs of a potential divorce war. Now I'd like to offer some "global" changes that would have the same impact on a much larger scale. Whether these suggestions will ever be implemented is debatable, but if they were, every divorcing couple would be better off:

Make premarital counseling a more accessible option

My dad once told me that bad communication was the cause of many divorces, and to highlight that fact, he added, "Women don't hear what men don't say." Certainly premarital counseling isn't a panacea for all the things that can go wrong in a marriage, but it certainly will help some couples to realize they should never get married and others to develop relationship problem-solving skills. People used to acquire marital communication skills and other relationship-building tools by observing their own parents. As I mentioned earlier, though, many people today may have been raised by parents who never got along and divorced before the kids were adolescents.

Premarital counseling should be akin to the classes couples attend before having a baby. They should simply help them acquire a few fundamentals that will help them make the difficulties and challenges of marriage manageable. In this way, even if couples do decide to divorce in the future, the tensions that have built up over all those years of marriage won't be as intense and will be less likely explode into a divorce war.

Implement a hybrid mediation/marital counseling process as soon as one person files for divorce

I've found that at least some marriages can be saved if people go through marital counseling as soon one partner files for divorce. The filing is often a wake-up call for the other spouse, and that may be exactly the reason the first spouse filed. More significantly, however, mediation and counseling can help dissolve a marriage without as much financial and emotional pain as would otherwise occur. This filing creates a crisis state; it mandates intervention early on, which can sometimes prevent the breakup of a family before a couple passes the point of no return. Through the hybrid process of mediation and counseling, couples can learn to debate issues without using the children as pawns. They can communicate all the frustration and hostility that they've harbored for years or haven't been conscious of without translating it into a long, costly divorce process. They can either save the marriage or divorce amicably.

Too often, people file for divorce and the fight begins immediately. Especially at the start, when the shock of the filing hits home, people aren't thinking clearly and begin litigating their marital issues. Friends, family, and the wrong type of gender-based groups can fuel this fighting, and it can quickly get out of control. Revenge, name-calling, and scheming become the focus rather than communication and healing.

The counseling/mediation hybrid approach I propose would provide couples with a cooling-down period if nothing else. Ideally, the mediator will also be a mental health professional with an understanding of the legal issues, in order to help people deal with their emotions as well as mediate subjects such as custody, visitation, maintenance, and division of assets. This would be a preliminary step prior to any litigation, but ideally, it will result in a saved marriage or an amicable divorce. As soon as attorneys join the fray, the process often becomes adversarial, and you don't want to communicate with your spouse via litigation.

Have your attorney review the mediated agreement and present it to the court for approval if the marriage can't be saved

After a couple goes through mediation successfully and decides to go forward with the divorce, the mediator should provide both attorneys with the agreement, and the attorneys should put the agreement in the proper legal form. Your attorney's role should be to make sure the agreement is fair. If it is, the attorneys present the agreement to the judge, who signs off on it, and the divorce is official.

Having a judge involved in the mediation process makes sense on two levels. If a judge is impartial, experienced, and has the benefit of the mediator's agreement, she is in an excellent position to help resolve whatever lingering disputes exist. The judge is seen by both parties as fair and authoritative, and the divorcing couple may be more inclined to listen to what she has to say under these circumstances, even if a great deal of anger exists between the parties.

Second, a judicial review at this point prevents some attorneys from exploiting the strong emotions one or both parties have and turning a relatively simple settlement case into a legal circus. It is said that when there is a $5 million estate in a divorce case, the wrong lawyer has five million reasons not to reach a quick settlement. An unethical lawyer knows he will lose a substantial amount of fees if he helps his client settle early, and so protects his financial interest by prolonging the settlement. Even an ethical lawyer may rationalize why prolonged negotiation and many court appearances are necessary, telling himself that if they "take it all the way," his client will receive better custody and financial results than if they agree on a compromise. Sometimes this last point is not a rationalization but the truth. Still, an early judicial review doesn't preclude moving forward; it simply provides another option for settlement and avoiding the financial and emotional hardships of a prolonged divorce.

Reeducate divorce attorneys

Lawyers are trained in combat. They are taught that the tougher they are, the harder the bargain they drive, the better the results for their clients. Consensus and compromise are anathema to many attorneys. This warrior stance might be appropriate in divorce cases under certain circumstances—when the other attorney's client is deranged and dangerous, for instance—but it is counterproductive in other situations. Especially when children are involved, lawyers need to take on the mediation function to a certain extent. They must realize that you can't win a divorce case when the kids "lose" one of their parents—when the process prevents them from seeing mom or dad regularly, or results in their being alienated from a parent. Kids lose, too, when the process turns parents vicious and they constantly bad-mouth the other parent or sabotage each other in some way.

It seems to me that everyone who practices family law should be required to pass a comprehensive certification class, one that would reeducate them about their role, especially when young children are part of the debate between parents. Experienced judges, other lawyers, and therapists should teach these classes, helping lawyers realize how much harm they do when they attempt to destroy their client's spouse, when they churn their fees, and when they don't make their best effort to achieve a settlement. They need to be reassured that they can still be tough and fight for the assets they believe their client deserves, but that when an issue involves children, they must learn to settle.

Even if no laws are passed mandating these recommendations, you can put them into effect in your own divorce.

Take advantage of counseling before and during your marriage. Work on communicating better and compromising when necessary.

Find attorneys who are willing to mediate first and litigate second. I realize that these attorneys are not always easy to find, but if you ask around, you'll probably find someone who will tell you about a lawyer who was compassionate, cared about the kids, and worked hard to settle even an ugly divorce case.

And that brings me to my last point. Even if your case is ugly, the information and suggestions in this book can make it manageable. By trying to avoid rubbing salt in your spouse's wound, by being willing to give up one thing to gain something else, by refusing to play dirty and file false accusations against your spouse as a negotiating ploy, you can deal effectively with at least some abusive, vengeful, or money-crazed spouses. Even when it comes to a divorce fight, you can fight fairly and intelligently by adhering to basic rules of human decency and legal protocols and win.

Above all else, when your divorce is on the verge of turning into a war, you need to focus your attention and that of your spouse on your children. A war is justified only if your spouse is cruel or irrational. If you are fighting to protect yourself or your kids, then you may need to fight with everything you have. Most of the time, though, spouses aren't cruel or irrational. Instead, they're angry, vengeful, paranoid, and fearful. To cut through these emotions and the negative repercussions they might have during a divorce, talk with your spouse about what's best for the kids. I have found that discussions of this type can prevent these emotions from dictating the course of a divorce. They encourage rationality and compromise.

By definition, divorce is an ugly business. In many instances, however, you can control how ugly it gets. You can confine the ugliness to a few weeks of arguments, a relatively small legal bill, and a tolerable amount of stress and emotional pain. For your kids' sake as well as your own, seek an end to the hostilities as quickly and painlessly as possible. My hope is that the information contained in these pages will help you achieve this objective.

INDEX